This book is to be returned on
or before the date stamped below

University of Plymouth Library
Subject to status this item may be renewed
via your Voyager account
http://voyager.plymouth.ac.uk
Tel: (01752) 232323

Against

Mine

Julia Jacquette, *Against Mine*, 1996. Enamel on wood, each panel 20x 20 in. Courtesy Holly Solomon Gallery, NYC.

First published 1997 by

Lusitania Press
104 Reade Street, NewYork, NY 10013
USA
A not-for-profit corporation

Editors: Martim Avillez, Saul Ostrow, Carole Ashley
Guest Editor: Allen S. Weiss
Design: Zhang Ga

Printed and bound in Hong Kong by Oceanic Graphic Printing, Inc.

ISBN 1-57027-080-5

Available through D.A.P./Distributed Art Publishers
155 Sixth Avenue, 2nd Floor, New York, NY 10013
Tel: 212-627-1999 Fax: 212-627-9484

This publication is made possible with public funds from the New York State Council
on the Arts, a State Agency.

TASTE
Nostalgia

EDITED BY ALLEN S. WEISS

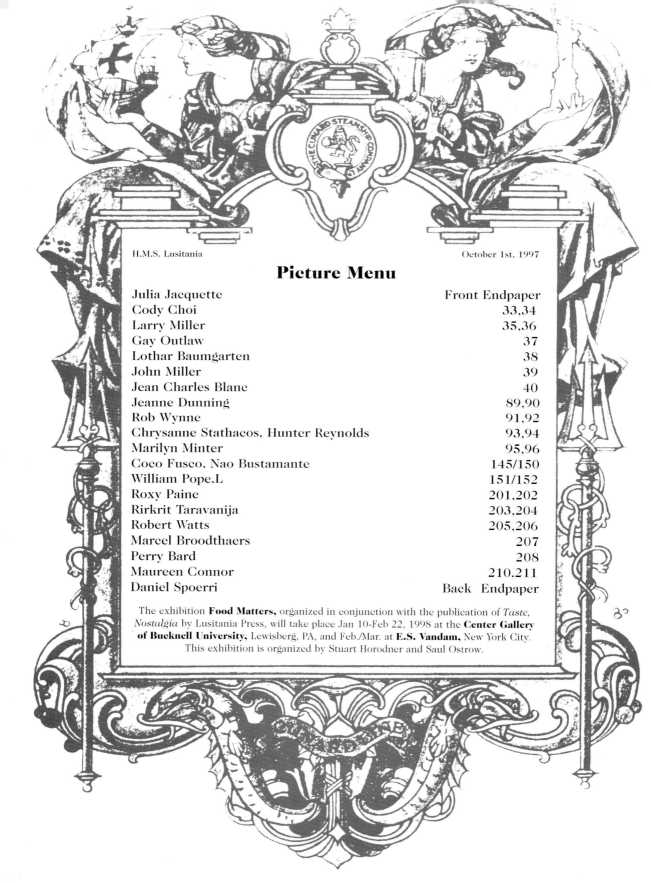

Picture Menu

The exhibition **Food Matters,** organized in conjunction with the publication of *Taste, Nostalgia* by Lusitania Press, will take place Jan 10-Feb 22, 1998 at the **Center Gallery of Bucknell University,** Lewisberg, PA, and Feb./Mar. at **E.S. Vandam,** New York City. This exhibition is organized by Stuart Horodner and Saul Ostrow.

Contents

**Nietzsche is not nourishment
—he is a stimulant**

Paul Valéry
Notebooks

Allen S. Weiss

Paradigms of Taste

for Corinne LaBalme

I was with de Kooning once in a restaurant and he said,
"If I put a frame around these bread crumbs, that isn't art."
And what I'm saying is that it is.

John Cage to Richard Kostelanetz
Conversing With Cage

The difficulty in discussing "taste" is not only due to the radical subjectiveness inherent in the cliché *de gustibus non est disputandum* (there is no disputing taste), but also to the lexical and epistemological equivocation of the word. Taste is simultaneously subjective, objective, and qualificative. According to context, *taste* means: the sense by which we distinguish flavors; the flavors themselves; an appetite for such preferred flavors; the discriminative activity according to which an individual likes or dislikes certain sensations; the sublimation of such value judgments as they pertain to art, and ultimately to all experience; and, by extension and ellipsis, taste implies good taste and style, established by means of an intuitive faculty of judgment. To conflate these determinations—with the attendant equivocations that such epistemological confusion might entail—is the only adequate entry into the poetics of cuisine and the philosophy of gastronomy.

The present project, organized under the sign of a hedonism both physical and metaphysical, is an attempt to unravel these ambiguities. Its ultimate goal is what Nietzsche saw to be the necessary condition of all true philosophy: the enhancement of life. For what is gastronomy if not a primal means of transforming necessity into pleasure?

One morning in the winter of 1978 brought the following exchange in the dining room of my eminently nondescript bed-and-breakfast at Cartwright Gardens in London:

"Coffee or tea?"
"Coffee."
"Cereal or eggs?"
"Eggs."
"How would you like them?"
"Over, please."
"Orange juice or bacon?"
Orange juice or bacon!? The shock of categorical incongruity
was an overture to future culinary discourse. Though it took
some time for the London lesson to sink in, Foucault's teachings
henceforth became of much more immediate import concerning
my reflections on the meaning of cuisine...

Soon after the publication of my book *Flamme et festin: Une
poétique de la cuisine* in 1994, I was invited to dinner in Paris:
a friend was arriving from Bordeaux with his trunk full of wine
and oysters—twelve dozen for the six of us. Pleased as I was by
the invitation, I mentioned, slightly embarrassed, that I wasn't
really fond of raw oysters, but I was assured that there would be
other things to eat, and in any case, my loss would be the oth-
ers' gain. After the apéritif, the friend—Emmanuel Grillet, pro-
prietor of Château Monichot of the Côtes de Bourg—excused
himself, saying that he had to prepare the oysters to be cooked
for the first course. With the exception of myself, everyone
seemed despondent at the thought of sacrificing oysters to the
flames. The oysters (*spéciales pied de cheval*) were opened, the
first and second waters eliminated, and the third water (the
purest) was mixed with an equal amount of Monbazillac (a
slightly sweet Bordeaux). The oysters were quickly poached in
the liquid mixture, placed back into their shells, and a spoonful
of heated crème fraîche was added, with a final turn of pepper.
It was brilliant.

This dish is of both gustatory and historical interest, as it is
mostly forgotten that at the turn of the century the French had
a predilection for drinking Sauternes and Barsac with oysters.
Thus, in contradistinction to the current preference for eating
oysters accompanied by very dry wines, this recipe bears the
trace of that superannuated taste. It establishes, in the culinary
domain, what Maurice Merleau-Ponty wrote of as an "under-
ground trading of the metaphor," opening up an entire gustatory
horizon.

In matters of taste, memory always interacts with history; idiosyncrasy is continually informed by typicality; names and cate-gories establish gustatory relations, kinships, limits, nuances. We find ourselves in a joyful hermeneutic circle where appreci-ation demands discrimination, while discrimination presuppos-es appreciation. The selectiveness of memory creates both iden-tities and differences, so that culinary idiosyncrasy is in the van-guard of invention, and any adequate answer to the question of taste must entail a discourse of inclusion, not exclusion; of open-ness, experimentation and risk, not reticence, denial and reac-tion. Thus a recipe is not a canon, code or regulation, and the typicality or "authenticity" of a dish is but a range of possibili-ties, an indeterminate ideal, a pole of transformations. Taste is the mark of a personal singularity that draws its sense from col-lective tradition, and its possibilities from continual creativity. This is not to discount tradition, but merely to historicize it, in the context of a hedonism that is a moveable feast.

In Greenwich Village there exists a legendary luncheonette whose specialty is soup. Nearly a hundred varieties are listed, most offered in ten degrees of spiciness, and many available in either meat-stock or vegetarian versions; multiplication creates a combinatory system of thousands of possibilities. Sesame, turnip, barley. Pear, walnut, spinach. Shrimp, spinach, bleu. It is as if this menu were an allegory of taste, where each soup is a rhetorical gesture that gives rise to reverie.

Taste is constituted simultaneously by recognition of typicality, judgment of quality, and choice of style—recognitions, judg-ments and choices often operative at infinitesimal, indeed sub-liminal, levels of determination. Taste as discrimination must be differentiated from taste as appreciation, even though the former is a necessary precondition of the latter. It might thus be fruitful to consider the question of taste according to a structural analy-sis, so as to contextualize the historical possibilities of choice without eliminating the problematic of idiosyncrasy. This menu illustrates the fact that, as in language, there are always more possibilities than might have been imagined, but not all combi-nations of elements are desirable. Not every point on the culi-nary combinatory grid has equal value; some are valueless, even nonsensical. But all nonsense, culinary and otherwise, is cultur-ally significant. To improve taste entails refining differentiations, distinguishing nuances, recognizing limits, elaborating codes, investigating histories and inventing relations, all the while upholding and occasionally intertwining those sundry traditions which are the very matrix of cuisine.

Taste constitutes a sign of individual style, a mode of constituting the self, a mark of social position, an aesthetic gesture. While inaugurating the most intimate pleasures, cuisine simultaneously offers an incontrovertible cultural façade; these pleasures and façades are founded and articulated by childhood nostalgia, eroticism, ethnography, and the virtuality at the core of the culinary imagination—the topics of *Taste, Nostalgia*. Here, against the solipsism, narcissism and phantasms of what would be the incommunicable idiosyncrasy of pure subjective taste, must be counterbalanced the communality, seduction and mythology of gastronomy.

CHILDHOOD NOSTALGIA

At the time
of the cholera epidemic,
in order to enlarge [the cemetery], a
part of the wall was destroyed and three
adjacent acres of land were bought. But this
entire new portion remains nearly uninhabited,
with the tombs, as in the past, continuing to be
crowded near the gate. The guardian, who is at the
same time grave-digger and church beadle (thus
obtaining a double profit from the corpses of the
parish), took advantage of the empty grounds in
order to plant his potatoes. However ,his little
field shrinks from year to year, and when
an epidemic takes place, he doesn't
know whether he should rejoice
because of the deceased or
grieve because of the
tombs.

Gustave Flaubert
Madame Bovary

Jeff Weinstein

White Toast and Butter

*i*t made him shake. It turned March's breakfast daylight into a scalpel's reflection. It made him transparent to time.

How does a little Brooklyn boy become "transparent"? He didn't know. But this seven-year-old, in his hospital bed, knew he was changed. He understood with an adult confidence that the dead toast and gelid butter on the tray in front of him would *become* him. For the first time in his life, his childishness dissolved in front of food.

The toast sat on a thick institutional plate, under a round stainless cover. Yet the vibrating boy could see through the metal, a secret Superman. And this Superman could do something else no one could: eat the toast before he ate it. Why couldn't he have managed this before? Where had he been?

A new hunger made this one boy two. Even as the old Jeff was, with his knife, dragging the square of hard fat across the limp burned bread, shearing its dark skin and uncovering bleached cotton underneath, the new Jeff was sniffing, chewing, tasting. A light-footed, empirical athlete was sent to run ahead of the regular boy, eating their food, possibly even enjoying it before the slower, younger one opened his mouth.

Anyone walking into the hospital room at this moment would see a slight child with glossy brown hair, deep brown eyes, and predictively sensual lips caught in the grip of insulin-generated tremors. The room was empty of people as far as the boy was concerned—and may well have actually been so. He couldn't recall, can't recall. He paid small attention, going back and forth into the peopled world at his leisure, because he had had his "brush with death."

To communicate their relief, his mom and dad told him the story of his brush with death the first day he opened his eyes: how he was snatched from the jaws of the operating room—where he was to have his appendix out—by one smart doc, who commanded he be given enormous injections of insulin over the next few days until some kind of equilibrium was reached.

("What's insulin? Can you get me a book?" the reborn Jeff asked immediately.) You were so sick, the operation would have killed you, his shocked parents said.

The boy was comatose during this mysterious "brush with death" and never felt the insulin needles. Yet the steer hormone forced his syrupy blood to burn up its long-collected "sugar": the capfuls of Seven-Up one murderously lazy doctor had prescribed every quarter hour to prevent dehydration; the well-meant Pyrex cups of My-T-Fine pudding and hefty slices of Ebinger's blackout cake he had been served as restorative treats in his parent's bed. The undiagnosed invalid, hardly knowing where he was, had seen time disappear under Mom's satin comforter. Later, in the hospital room, in front of something as simple, as banal, as cold toast and butter, time reappeared. But it was a different time, a double time, fast and clear. Jeff's brand-new clock was wound by a crazy, insulin-flogged hunger, and his sense of time was replaced by a sense of food.

I suppose it's time to talk about the taste of that toast, because it's taste was tested on a perfectly clean palate, in a virgin mind. The boy who was supposed to be me can still recall the flavor, and I think he can remember it accurately in the midst of that brittle sunshine, in a mechanical bed too high off the floor. But this flavor has been fighting for its life and primacy for so many years that I expect it has dragged any likely details along with it, no matter if they're true or false. Some flavors are desperate.

And it doesn't help that this flavor, like all its significant future cohorts, will not be bound by words. It couldn't be bound then, and will not be now. I'll try some, to show you: *Rubbery. Carbonized and crummy. Sodden from steam. Sad.*

You know why these don't work? Because the toast was the best thing I have ever eaten. It was so good that I never forgot it. Or is it that because I never forgot it, it was so good? This is what critics mean when they write that something is momentous. The toast's merit, weighed against a rich, luscious challah at B & H Dairy on Manhattan's Second Avenue; or against a sinful seeded rye little Jeff carried home from the bakery in a waxed paper bag, sneaking variously sized slices from every part of the loaf in the hope no one would perceive a gap; or against the fermentative aroma of the first, fallen loaf of French bread big Jeff baked under his friend Kit's direction; or against this piece of routine Italian bread I am about to pop between my lips right now... such calibrated merit falls into a trough of relativity, never to stand by itself. Hunger determines merit. Hunger alone. Every critic should have this etched onto his or her daily mirror. It is the basis of humanistic evaluation.

I could probably say that I became a restaurant critic because of cold toast. Cold toast, that is, plus insulin. The practical coincidences that led me away from the biology lab and the literature faculty lounge and toward my first newspaper column are ancillary. Pardon the redundancy, but fate is unavoidable. I am a food writer because I am a diabetic.

I said it. In fact, I said it with the article, the a, acknowledging the centrality of insulin to my identity. Whether I like it or not, and whether it's correct or not, I am a diabetic, not just "diabetic." This is what happens when an impressionable youngster is offered a word that allows him to choose between adjective or noun: between a hat or a face. Diabetes—so much less personal a word—is not a condition laminated over you, something that colors your mood like a biological scrim. It is part and parcel of you, the body-and-mind you, just the way your race or gender is. It can be challenged, subsumed, or ignored, but it remains the residual, basal you.

I should admit that my belief may result merely from a language accident of the past. As a child, I was asked by one of my doctors to carry around a wallet card that read; "I Am a Diabetic. I Have Not Been Drinking." Confused? Imagine me. Imagine, as I had to, a grade-school Jewish boy from Midwood, Brooklyn, walking the streets drunk. He wasn't even allowed to walk the streets sober, to ride the subway, to be out by himself after dark. I read this card over and over. "I am..." What kid has a card saying he *is*? The line on the card became practical poetry to me, poetry whose syntax and deadpan defensiveness I have never entirely put aside.

The card was supposed to excuse my slurred speech and irrational actions during an insulin reaction, the result of a dose of insulin not perfectly matched by a measured amount of food eaten at the proper time, or made more potent by unusual exercise. Little Brooklyn boys are notorious for taking unplanned sprints across the school yard, escaping bullies.

The worst thing about an insulin reaction is that the insulin sneaks up rapidly and bypasses ordinary hunger: you begin to starve without having known the pleasure of anticipating food. The best thing about an insulin reaction was its '50s antidote: something sweet. Here is the agreed-upon list of generic answers to a "reaction": juice, candy, soda, cookies. But young hunger is never generic. Was there more life in the Lifesavers—how apt— I carried in my pocket, or in their rival holeless Charms? My palate disposed of these confetti flavors so quickly that I graduated to Callard & Bowser butterscotch, thrilled that butter and sugar could conjoin in anything so translucent and solid. Why did I finish that box of Lorna Doone's in the doctor's office when I knew that only one or two would do the trick? (I'll tell you why. Because hunger is more persuasive than knowledge.)

A friend of my father's who owned a Manhattan luncheonette gave us an unmarked quart bottle of brogue-brown Coca-Cola syrup, the easier for me to swig when I felt "one" coming on. Tasting Coke syrup is not the same as tasting Coke; the process feels simultaneously primitive and modern, like drinking the blood of commerce. I kept a small glass vial of this elixir close to me for a year, refilling when necessary. My own private Coke. It completely replaced my taste for normal Coke, which became a sissy dilution.

None of my friends carried Coke syrup around; none, apparently, had reason to think beyond the fizz. The few I showed my treasure to were envious, or pretended to be, and I relished their envy, or at least their attentiveness. However, I relished even more the information I alone was heir to about the essence of common things. Attention and information: being a diabetic had its compensations. Everything edible would disclose its agenda and effect. They were mine to discover. When food is medicine, you never want the illness to disappear.

Blancmange with Almond Milk

The Froth of the Waves

"Stop playing with the foam," shouted Sonia's grandmother, tired of seeing us endlessly return to her, our faces covered with froth, all in tears because of the salt that burned our eyes. We had the look of someone who just escaped, right in the middle of a shave, from a demon barber. We weren't sorry. All we wanted was that she get rid of all the foam, sometimes mixed with fine strands of seaweed, that clogged our noses, mouths and eyes.

Right afterwards we once again ran along the sea shore. And the game recommenced. We walked the length of the beach in the frothy water, scooping up that weightless whiteness, chatting innocently, and then suddenly one of us would dump it all on the other's head. That announced a furious combat. The first one to cry "uncle!" was the loser. She had swallowed too much water, and she could neither breathe nor see. She had bitten the froth of the waves.

The Host

"Open your mouth wide," said the priest, "stick out your tongue, and the instant you receive the sacred host pay strict attention so that it doesn't touch your teeth. Listen carefully: your teeth must not even so much as graze the body of our Father." Marlene, who had a large set of braces on her teeth, was terrified; and I, even without this handicap, was filled with anxiety. Each Sunday I prepared to take communion with the idea that something dreadful was going to happen. "Imagine," I told Sonia, "that I bite into a son of God and that he begins to bleed in my mouth."

"*The* son of God," she corrected me.

"Whether or not he is an only child makes no difference at all concerning the blandness of the thing."

"Who knows. But it's true. It is bland. Tasteless."

"It's so that nobody refuses communion under the pretext that he doesn't like the taste. Or inversely, to avoid gluttons who sneak back on line several times to have their fill."

"I like that blandness. The manner in which the host gets soft and dissolves, without one's encountering any substance whatsoever."

"Shut up. You disgust me."

Sonia was fanatical about that white glue that tasted like almonds, with which she stuffed herself. She also delighted in Nestlé's milk, especially because of the tube. As for me, I didn't like any of that. On the other hand, I loved to leave communion, hands joined, eyes lowered, all my senses keen to feel the insipid and divine pellicle vanish against my tongue. There existed a perfect moment, when I turned my back to the altar and begin to walk down the central aisle, just as I imagined the host still intact, a minuscule moon at the opening of my throat, gently bringing light to the depths of my body.

Yoghurt of Grated Stone

My mother, for whom the kitchen was always the site of her most

awful anger (she sometimes hurled pots and pans against the opposite wall, precisely the wall of Sonia's house), had for some time been equipped with a bizarre round thing that was supposed to make yoghurt. It was clear that she controlled it poorly. Since the apparition of this machine, the only thing I ever got for dessert was liquidy and granulous yoghurt. I would ingurgitate it in one big swallow and then quickly leave to play outside, where Sonia and Michel, the neighbor from the house facing ours, awaited me.

A white and tender stone was needed. We scraped it against the concrete floor of the courtyard. When we had a sufficient quantity, we gathered it together in a small heap which we spilled into a yoghurt container with the aid of a spoon. We added water and stirred. We drew lots to see who would taste it. The chosen one fled at top speed. The pursuit could last a long time, but in the end the victim was always caught, and condemned to submission. Vanquished as he or she may be, the victim seemed resolved not to submit to the vile brew—mouth tightly closed, and too bad if we spilled the yoghurt all over the victim's face, hoping that this would force the mouth open. Which is precisely what would happen, such that a few drops of ground stone yoghurt were swallowed. The unlucky one trembled with disgust and always found the force to be liberated from the tormentors. Then it was their turn to flee and to run with all their might. But sometimes it happened that one of them slipped on the puddle of yoghurt and fell down. What followed was atrocious.

Blancmange with almond milk on a strawberry coulis

Those games which mix whiteness, taste and disgust, laughter and fear, are long gone. They suddenly came to mind, one lovely May evening, because of my choice of dessert in a Parisian restaurant. The menu offered a large range of pleasures, but without any hesitation I chose a blancmange with almond milk on a strawberry coulis. It arrived in the form of a beautiful ring of opal, freshly turned out of the mold, and set on a deep red sauce. The essence of a sunset. I was very careful not to spread the sauce on the almond jelly. I waited a long time before I dared touch it, first with my tongue, then with my teeth. Its milky, silky smoothness and melting contact thrilled me. I closed my eyes: a perfect childrens' food, emerging from a chaos of violence and repulsion, from wild desires and an unbridled imagination, now pacified. A phantom isle upon which I softly alight...

Translated by Allen S. Weiss

Yes, I ate
fire, I ate its goldness,
its aroma and even its sparkle
as the burning hot waffle crunched
between my teeth. And it's always like
this, by a sort of enjoyment of luxuries,
such as dessert, that fire reveals its humanity.
It doesn't confine itself to cooking: it makes
crisp. It gilds the crust. It materializes men's
feasts. As far back as one goes, gastronomic
value, and it is in joy rather than in need that
man discovered his spirit. The conquest of
the superfluous offers greater spiritual
excitation than the conquest of
necessity. Man is a creation
of desire, not a creation
of need.

Gaston Bachelard
The Psychoanalysis of Fire

Richard Schechner

Sab's Hot Dogs

Not every Sunday night, but almost, especially in winter, my mother, wondering what to feed us as the weekend closed, got the bright idea of sending one of us boys down to Sab's to get hot dogs, six of 'em, two for each of us. Redolent with sauerkraut, mustard-blanketed, with sweet green pickle relish or bitingly hot, nose-juice-inducing red hot pepper sauce, enticingly wrapped in soft creamy colored buns, their slits just barely parted to lovingly embrace but not conceal or even fully contain in their pre-pubescent vulvas six tightly skinned elongated uncircumcised yet Jewish phalluses, mouth-watering and appetizing beyond imagining, hot dogs. During the week we ate suppers of lightly breaded fried filet of flounder or sweet and sour cabbage piled next to meatloaf (which smelled goodly warm and substantial like my mother's shit, or was it the other way round, the maternal shit smelling as luxurious as meatloaf lapped in gravy?), or sometimes, on fancy nights, lamb chops or, at the other extreme, a boiled vegetable-only meal of beets, potatoes, string beans—even, horror of horrors! okra, as slimy green as warm snot. Hard to believe that in my declining years. okra is a favorite, its slippery substance reminding me of you know what. These non-Sunday repasts were nourishing and even enjoyable.

But Sunday night was different. The smell of the hot dogs would get to me a long time before I ended the race down Renner Avenue to Elizabeth Avenue, turn left and further down the hill, past the red brick twelve story high apartment buildings—oh, how unlucky were those apartment dwellers, thought my eleven-year old soul, living flattened on one floor, in two dimensions only, with no basement to escape to, no upper story with its piles of boxes and grandpa's study loaded with secrets inside his desk, where I peeked, later when I was twelve or thirteen, to find a packet of photos of naked or nearly so burlesque girls, all smiles and tits. This discovery, so shocking, so terribly appetizing to a young boy's eyes and penis, was to have lifelong repercussions, setting me searching avenues of pornography, always of the safest kind, the least kinky, the most benign "girl next door" kind, the little-girl-you-know-who-fucks kind. But that was later, when my exile had already begun and Sab's was forever out of reach, I having earned no visa back to the old country.

"Rich," my mother said, "here's three dollars for six hot dogs. boiled, not grilled, don't forget." Boiled are better, cleaner, safer, mommy says so. And all through my life since whenever I crunch into a grilled hot dog I experience on my tongue and in the interior of my mouth, in the cracks between my teeth and over the smooth surfaces of my cheeks, the taint and pleasure of dirt, grease, and grime. I feel my mother's reproach (though she later enjoyed charcoal grilled dogs, where the grease drops below and flares up in the flames. The injunction thou shalt boil thy hot dogs must have come to my mother via her father, the pharmacist, my grandpa to whom boiling meant sterilizing. At Sab's I saw the clean dogs, tumescent sausages, smooth turds, red-brown penises, tantalizing tidbits mouth-ready, rising falling turning in the boiling waters. Except for these Sunday night indulgences, hot dogs were pretty much food forbidden us. Not Kosher, not healthy, not available. So it was with a rush of inflamed appetite that I flew down the Renner Avenue hill, banked the Elizabeth Avenue corner, and wheeled left again at Meeker. Gulping big breaths as I entered the homestretch, I zoomed past The Tavern Restaurant, a fancy WASP eatery where, as soon as you sat down, the waiters automatically brought you in a clear glass dish celery and olives over crushed ice and a sterling bread tray with crusty salt sticks wrapped in white linen napkins, the same as were stood up in a fan as part of each diner's setup. The Tavern was where my father's immigrant father, ostentatious and glorious with his American wealth, sometimes brought us for Saturday or Sunday midday dinner, a real treat, but also a chore because I was required to dress up in a suit and tie and keep my mouth shut while eating. To this day my wife rebukes me for talking with my mouth full.

Sab's was in the dip a block beyond The Tavern, under the twin bridges over which rushed the traffic of Route 22 on one span and the Lehigh Valley Railroad on the other. Not exactly a prime location in terms of view. Coming down Meeker, Sab's was on the right, really not much of a place architecturally speaking. Sab's consisted of a walkup counter and to the side of that about five or six tables where you could sit and eat if that was your pleasure. No waitress service, just the opportunity for respite. This part of the establishment was open to the street in the summer and closed in during winter. From their position behind the counter, Sab the fat proprietor, his fat wife, and his fat sons could see nothing but traffic and the concrete abutments of the railroad and highway bridge. Traffic was heavy and business good as people for miles around desired Sab's high quality kosher beef dogs. Even families long since migrated to the Oranges or Short Hills or even Livingston would repatriate to Sab's—that is, until after 1967, the Newark riots, and the transformation of Weequahic from a Jewish to a black ghetto.

In the gloam of a December Newark Sunday night, the cold against my fingers, the icy air biting the inside of my nostrils, the sight—and smell!—of Sab's was better than heaven herself. And was I lucky! No one was ahead of me. I would get served tout de suite. I rushed to the counter. On the cool side of the grill were about ten dogs awaiting execution. Next to the grill was the boiling pot, lid closed. Sab himself was manning the helm. Roly-poly, almost as wide as he was high, ruddy, balding, with fat Jew-lips, meaty and lascivious, Sab eyed me. "Yeah? What can I do for you, kid?" Sab really didn't know me from Adam. "Two sweet works, one hot works, one mustard kraut, and two mustard. Boiled." "Boiled?" "Boiled." I waved the three bucks at him so he knew I wasn't going to welsh on the order. Even as he opened behind him the door of the white looks-like-a-home-fridge but a lot bigger, reaching his fat hand in to grab a half dozen dogs, dumping them without looking and without missing into the vat of turbulent fat-speckled broth, Sab reconfirmed my order in unpunctuated Newarkese: "Two sweet two mustard a hot an' a mustard kraut boiled right?" Nothing if not fresh. No dogs already swimming. Everything made to order. "Right" as I forked over the three bucks. "Boiled, Yeah." Before leaving the house I had taken my orders. Two dogs for each of us boys. Nothing for mom or pop. This was our treat, our Sunday night special. As I waited there in the growing darkness, the busy traffic of Meeker Avenue rolling behind me, the traffic lights changing steadily green yellow red, red green, green yellow red, red green, I inhaled the dogs.

I can taste that smell now, a half-century later. It makes me salivate today as I did then, Pavlov's dog, chained to that underpass, forever and ever (as the CD of Handel's *Messiah* is orating to me even as I type in these words, in Taipei Taiwan a number of universes from that Sunday night Newark circa 1945). Waiting on one foot and then on the other, it always took too long. Why didn't Sab know I was on my way? Why didn't he have those dogs already in the boiling vat. Why didn't he have them all ready for me so that as soon as my little boy's face pressed over the counter he'd push the dogs at me singing, "Hey, Richie, where ya been? Here ya go!" as he delivered into my clutch the box of six steaming hot powerful smelling mouth watering dogs. I demand now as then immediate gustatory satisfaction. Which it is not my lot in life to get.

So you can imagine the trouble I had running home with the dogs—running home and not eating them, not nibbling into this one or that one. Well, I cheated of course. I took a string of steamy kraut from one, pinched a tail of gut-covered hot dog skin from another, stroking the juicy meat across the yellow Gulden's mustard (no Grey Poupon in those plebeian days) and tasted the strong smell on my fingers. A cunt of kraut, a vagina-juice of mustard, a labia of buns: I was all desire as I ran back up the street, looking up now and then at the lights outlining the rectangles of windows in the apartment house across from our mansion, the place where Bill Greenfeld lived, the fattest man I knew, always huffing puffing sweating when he arrived at our house for pinochle with my father and grandpa. Or the shoddier apartment where the Gourd lived, the only corn-stalked haired boy I knew. His family name was Hay (of course! of course), and he was Scots. Not a Jew and my best friend—even the thought of it was dangerous, and fun. Gourd and I hung out a lot and set fires. More about that later, the adventures of the neighborhood incendiaries. As I set my feet on the long flight of steps up from Renner to the front terrace of my house and then tearing around the side of the house past the sunparlor with its floor to ceiling windows à la an Italian or French

manor house (what did my mother's father have in mind when he built that house?), and finally up the back porch stairs to face the back door.

Now here's a dilemma. I am carrying the hot dogs in their steamy box, with two hands, I am mad with hunger, even more aroused after stealing some fragments of flavor. (Did I some weeks actually take a bite into one of my own dogs? Would I have permitted myself that? How bad could a boy get?) Balancing the box on my right arm I twisted the knob with my left, being left-handed, and opened the door into the kitchen. It was steamy in there. The kitchen windows were covered with condensation. I could sketch with my forefinger on those steamy windows. Suddenly everything beyond the kitchen was obliterated. There was no outside once I was inside. My mother had set the kitchen table. No dining room for Sab's dogs, for Sunday night kids only supper. In a long handled pot on the stove were Van Camp's Vegetarian Baked Beans. No pork rind, no lard here. Where were my brothers? Do I have to wait for them to conclude this hungry narrative? Aren't the dogs theirs as well as mine? I don't want to share even the memory of Sab's Sunday night boiled dogs with them. I want all six dogs for myself; I want the whole table, my mother, the entire house, the universe for myself.

But that's not real, my brothers were there, plenty. Do I dare give their real names? Do they have real names? None of us have real names, or hardly any of us do. We have the names bestowed on us by family history, by parental desire, by convention. Anyway, for this time being these brothers of mine will remain nameless. I don't have the stomach to nominalize them, it is enough that I enumerate them: oldest number 1, next oldest number 2. And youngest number 4 not yet born; so he doesn't count, though by this time he was four years old. Why then is he excluded? Why did I not buy him at least one hot dog? Didn't he deserve one, plain maybe, cut into small bite-size pieces by my mother. OK, maybe there were seven dogs brought home. But how does that compute into the three dollars, the 50 cents per dog? It doesn't. And let's leave it at that. My youngest brother doesn't figure in, either nominatively or in terms of financial arithmetic. As for my father, the less said about him at this moment the better.

So we sit down at the table, those of us there are, three or four; and my mother hovers over and around us dishing out from a bowl the baked beans, a single spoonful here two there, according to our sizes and our expressed appetites. We drink soda, ginger ale or coca-cola, poured from a single large bottle; or do we each have small individual bottles? Do we have sodas at all? Maybe just water. Certainly not milk, in that kosher home. It all begins to fade. What happens in the house once the hot dogs are delivered I get back by means of logical

reconstruction not powerfully envisioned memory. I see Sab's as clear as one of those great bigger than life Diego Rivera murals in Mexico city. I envision that little fat man in his white butcher's apron (meat's his game, after all), his bright brown eyes dancing in his red face, his tongue flogging those meaty red Arab lips (did I say Jew before?), his commanding position superior to his grill, a colossus astride his vat of boiling delicatessen. And smell the hot dogs cooking in the vat, watch Sab impale them on his never-failing extra long fork. I anticipate the taste of those dogs as Sab inserts them into their buns, anoints them with sweet and hot relish, mustard, the works. I see this rabbi of frankfurter present his work to me across the counter, snug in their box ready for the journey back up the hill. All that with a clarity that belongs to a memory painted with the longest lasting photo-real acrylic. But the scene inside the house, my birth-house, the drama of actual consumption, that's not so clear. There all is as blurry as Impressionism, a Monet, or is it Manet, perceived through a scrim. I know I could work it out, squeezing the screen memory out of my brain, point by colored point. And I will.

Terri Kapsalis

Yiayia's Hands

*e*xplosions preserve remarkable details. Consider the island of Thera, also known as Santorini, where the Greek version of Pompeii was found. Lava from a furious volcanic eruption that ripped the island in half stilled this part of Minoan civilization around 1500 B.C. In 1967, archeologists unearthed the Minoans' three-storied houses and pottery. A successful fisherman, boxing boys, frolicking monkeys, a bodice-less woman were frozen in color wall paintings.

Yiayia is a cook of explosions and crises. She is urgent among sputtering oils, paring knives, and hot ovens. Each encounter a potential disaster to be overcome before the dish can be completed. Thick sea salt like broken glass is ground into her hard, red hands as she rubs them together over her creation. The same with dried oregano stalks fetched from a steel canister. Whole twigs are stripped and crushed, stinging fingers and palms, releasing oregano bursts. No delicate temperatures. Food bubbles furiously in submission. Her hands are her hot pads. Deep frying is most alarming. When making *loukoumades*, fried doughballs soaked in melted honey, her hands hover above the boiling oil. She squeezes out dough ovals. As they slide into the oil, it responds with an upward blurp, burning her hands. No break for soothing ice or cold water. Explosions and crises are built into her recipes. There are no index cards or folded, stained papers. The recipes are written into her hands, into the strata of her calluses. Oregano shards, lemon dust, fossilized garlic essence, petrified olive oil.

> We assemble the moussaka, layer by layer. In the
> casserole we place the first layer, eggplant slices
> that have been browned in hot oil.

Her hands were once soft. The soft hands she hid behind her
father when a neighbor man demented by syphilis came to pro-
pose that she be his wife. She was raised in a fishing village in
Mani. The land was hard—mounds of bleached rock, low scrub-
by bushes and gnarled olive trees. But her softness contradicted
her setting. She was the most beautiful daughter of the village's
most important man. He was a trader and importer. He had a
store that sold the villagers clothes and tools and food. Her sis-
ter worked in the store. But she did not. She had a fine life. She
would dive off cliffs into the sea. Her fingers broke through the
smooth salt. The soft core of her pre-nuptial hands cured by the
sea. Early elegance.

We take a small fishing boat or *kaiki* to the site. It is the only
way to get there. A vast cave by the sea. This is where the
archeo-logy professor did his graduate digs. We wander the cave,
looking into the cool pools and at the collapsed rock. He takes us
to the rectangle of missing earth. One at a time we climb into the
deep crypt. The layers have been labeled with markers. The stri-
ations are tidy and discrete. Large stretches of time and scores
of events compressed into single centimeters. The smell of old
soil. The professor points to one particular level. "There it is.
The earliest evidence of fire."

Noosed dead bodies litter the streets. Exploding shops. Black
market vegetables. Hunger, starvation, and the German occupa-
tion. "It was the olive oil. It saved us." Yiayia always says. They
had olive oil from her village. Only small amounts, but this
murky green liquid gold kept them from starving. They also had
a little bread made from carob flour or *ksilokerato*, meaning
"wood-horn." Sometimes there was *horta* or greens, usually dan-
delion. Yiayia and her sister used the dregs of the olive oil mixed
with lye to make soap for cleaning bodies and clothes and
homes.

> On top of the eggplant we spread the meat fla-
> vored with onions, tomato, parsley, cinnamon
> and wine, laced with eggs and cheese.

Her thick fingers and hardened palms are no longer receptive
sensors. They are cutting boards, measuring cups, scrapers,
mortar and pestle. To excavate the layers would reveal a cata-

logue of artifacts: lemon infused animal fats, boiling honey, and the Virgin Mary's lamp oil. Sediment from twisted rugs, aired sheets, heated irons, scrub rags, and sweet grains prepared for the dead.

> On top of the eggplant we spread the meat flavored with onions, tomato, parsley, cinnamon and wine, laced with eggs and cheese.

My cousins and aunt and I urge her to wait, "Perimena, Yiayia," until the intestines cool. Having boiled in water with oil, they are slippery and keep their heat. But, she won't listen, driven to prepare the *mageritsa*, the special Easter stew that must be eaten just after Christ has risen. Her hands dance with the intestines in an attempt to cut efficiently while attempting to manage the heat. "Yiayia," we all scold persistently at high volumes and pitches as we watch her thick hands get redder. Her kitchen shears snip little pieces off the long intestines. "Before I had the scissors, this was very difficult work," she explains. "With a knife it takes for ever. Plus these intestines have already been cleaned. When I was young, we had to clean them. What difficult work." Every Easter and at choice moments in between my father shares familiar scatological *mageritsa* anecdotes. About the stench in the kitchen. About the intestine that hadn't been cleaned so thoroughly. He finds this line between food and excrement entertaining. When the intestines are cool enough to handle, Yiayia hands over the shears to my aunt who continues to snip until my twelve year old cousin successfully begs to play her part in this important stew. The shears are too big for her hands, but she snips away religiously.

Papou peels fruit like an aristocrat. Sitting at the kitchen table, his back is straight, neck angled. His thumb and fingers work with an exaggerated exactitude. He makes you believe that nothing could be more important or dignified than that job of he who pares. As he does his work, he may tell you about the glories of ancient Greece and of Christianity, the two now melded in his mind as though Zeus and Jesus were crucified side by side in the shadows of the Parthenon. Carefully peeling each apple, orange, peach, or pear, he herds the skins into a neat pile and pushes it towards Yiayia. She places one hand at the table's edge and sweeps the peels into it. Papou slowly eats his raw accomplishment.

> Above the meat layer we lay more eggplant slices side by side.

The nearby archeologists dismantle the Parthenon one piece at a time, replacing each stone with a recently fashioned replica. The pollution eats the hard stones. The rumble of the overhead planes nibble at history. So the artificial will be proudly displayed evidence of the birth of Western civilization. Its double retiring to quiet archival confinement

Out of the crowded airport and into the blinding sun and dry heat. Met with kisses and carnations. Then stuffed into a car too small for the number of passengers. Screeching and honking through the Athens highways. Dodging motorbikes and pedestrians under the hovering smog, each time thicker and darker than the last visit. Up to Yiayia and Papou's apartment. All velvet and needlepoint. Straight to the kitchen and into the icebox for *krema karamela*. There it is in a small metal cup with its cousins on a round lipped tray. A dull knife is used to circumnavigate the cup. The sound of scraping metal on metal. Then a saucer is placed upon it and the saucer-cup team inverted. As the cup is lifted, light brown caramel tumbles down a smooth cream custard which retains its cup shape. Eating air infused with light, cool and sweet. The toasted sugar caramel reminiscent of smoking wood.

> On top of the eggplant we apply another layer of
> meat mixture.

Is it a coincidence that her eyesight began to fail rapidly when he insisted that his diet consist of a strange overboiled thin pasta mush, creamed into milk, and then scooped up with chunks of old, dry bread? He declared this *fide* to be his salvation. While

she prepared it diligently for him every afternoon until she could no longer see the burner dials, this dish was an insult to her hands. Soft and pale and flavorless. Papou says it is good for his digestion. "I am a small child," he declares time and again from ninety-five year old lips. His statement is not altogether untrue. He philosophizes endlessly about this curious life cycle where old man and small child become one with the stars and the universe and beyond.

> When all the eggplant and meat have been exhausted we top them with an eggy béchamel—thick and smooth.

Filo must be handled at a steady pace, not too rushed or the delicate sheets might rip, but not too slow or the dough will dry out, become hopelessly fragile, and break. Like making a bed, each layer of filo is held up high with two hands. Wrists are curled under and flicked forward so that the air irons wrinkles and makes the dough horizontal. Hands are then quickly lowered, filo resting at the bottom of the buttered casserole. A brush with melted butter paints the sheet. And then another is added in the same manner. Butter is brushed again. Six more times at which point filling is added. This step decides the flavor and name of the dish—*tyropita, spanakopita, kreatopita, manataropita, galaktoboureko, baklava*. Above the filling another sheet of filo, brushed butter. Seven more times. Then a final layer of brushed butter. With a knife, the filo is scored, and cold water is lightly sprinkled. The heat of the oven melds butter and filo, while giving each sheet a unique color and character. The top layer is the darkest golden brown, crispiest, and most unruly looking. Its

dramatic waves form sculptural peaks. This top layer is also the one most tempting to a child lurking about the cooling master-piece. It is possible to break off pieces of this very top layer with-out anybody knowing. For sometimes it cracks of its own accord during baking, the fractured top sheet barely discernible from the layer beneath since that second-from-the-top sheet is only slightly lighter in color and crispness than the one above it. If she is particularly successful, the child might eventually escape with the whole top layer, popping each scrap of golden crisp into her mouth while she works in order to dispose of the evidence. She will not chew openly or the crunch will sound like an alarm. Rather she will place each piece on her tongue like a welcome sacrament and close her mouth, keeping it still. Without the movements of teeth and tongue to begin the preliminary churn of digestion, the filo flake will take matters into its own hands, summoning saliva with a sharp, almost stinging sensation which eventually rewards by turning soft and buttery. At the table where she can perform her delicate operations openly and with-out threat of interruption, she will excavate each layer, munch-ing audibly as she goes down to the two just above the filling. At this level, the sheets become delicate, moist, and chewy.

> On top of the béchamel we sprinkle a handful of
> grated cheese and then bake.

With her sight now gone completely, Yiayia mourns the days when the kitchen was hers. She cries as she recounts a list of the dishes she used to make. Her hands are grasped together, solac-ing one another as if they are having an agonizing memory of their own. But even with her sight gone completely, occasional-ly a dish miraculously appears from the kitchen—*pastitsio* or *domates me avga* prepared by hands that remember.

What form will the final explosion take? The last crisis? And what exquisite traces will remain?

Cody Choi, *Golden Boy Poster (yellow),* 1987-93. C-print 11in x 14 in. Collection A. G. Rosen.

Cody Choi, *The Thinker*, December #3, 1996. Toilet paper, Pepto-bismol, wood. 44 x 36 x 111 in. Courtesy Deitch Projects, NYC.

Larry Miller. *A Cross*, 1969. Bitter-sweet chocolate.

Larry Miller, *A Cross, Melting*, 1969-70, installation in Douglass Gallery show. Nailed to wall, melted during show (1970).

Gay Outlaw, *Mille Feuilles*, 1992. Flour, butter, salt, 14 x 30 x 11 in.

Lothar Baumgarten, *The Origin of Table Manners*, 1971. C. Print, 18-15/16 x 23-1/2 in.
Courtesy Marian Goodman Gallery, NYC.

John Miller, *The Office Party and The Comunist Party*, 1991. Mixed media. 47-1/4 x 39-1/4 x 11-3/4 in.
Courtesy Metro Pictures, NYC.

Jean Charles Blanc, *Captain Cook's Sardines*. (Tahiti), 1997.

The most peculiar articles of exchange that they offered us were human heads and hands, not yet completely stripped of their flesh, which they had eaten, (...). And, one could in effect state without any doubt that some of them had been exposed to fire. There was therefore justification in believing that the horrible custom of feeding themselves with the flesh of their enemies reigned among these natives.

In the *Journal of Captain James Cook*, dated March 30, 1778, an account of the first day of his visit to the Island of Nootka — Island of Vancouver, B.C.

In March 1978, the Ottawa Government commemorated the bi-centennial of the discovery of Nootka by the English navigator. At the festivities organized on the Island, at Friendly Cove, with British and Spanish guests, the Indian tribes of Nootka made a very remarkable entrance: men, women and children were dressed for the occasion in T-shirts on which were printed: **Cook, the Captain**.

APHRODISIA

One day, the Prince de Soubise had the intention of throwing a party, which would end with a supper, for which he requested the menu. Upon awakening the next day, his maître d'hôtel gave him a lovely show-card ornamented with vignettes, and the item which caught the Prince's glance was the following: fifty hams. "Really, Bertrand," he said, "I think that fifty hams is outrageous! Do you want to feed my entire regiment?"

"Non, my Prince, only one will appear on the table, but the rest is no less necessary for my sauce espagnole, my stocks, my trimmings, my..."

"Bertrand, you're robbing me, and I won't permit this purchase!"

"Ah! Your Highness," said the artist, hardly able to restrain his anger, "you don't understand our resources! Just give the order, and I shall make these fifty hams that offend you enter into a crystal flask no larger than your thumb."

Jean-Anthelme Brillat-Savarin
The Physiology of Taste

Lawrence R. Schehr

Rossini's Castrati

master of timing, genius of the classical opera, Gioacchino Rossini stopped writing opera with the failure of his *William Tell* after its 1829 premiere and devoted himself thereafter to a life of sybaritic pleasure. For the remaining four decades of his life he merely trifled with music from time to time; he produced no more operas and wrote only two more masterpieces, the *Stabat Mater* and the *Petite Messe Solennelle*. When asked in 1860, some thirty years after his retirement, by no less important a visitor than Richard Wagner, why he had stopped writing opera, Rossini told him that the art of singing had faltered. And what, pursued Wagner, led to this deterioration? Rossini's answer was simple; he attributed the decline of the art to "the disappearance of the castrati."[1]

Times had changed and perhaps left him behind, but before that, time had always been a friend to Rossini. The stories about Rossini and time are copious. First comes the famous anecdote of Rossini's purported laziness. Stendhal tells the story of Rossini writing a duet for *Il Figlio per azzardo*.[2] It was winter and Rossini was safely nestled under the covers of his bed. The duet he had just written fell on the floor, and Oblomov-like, too lazy to get out of bed—or more charitably, too unwilling to risk the cold room—Rossini decided not to retrieve the lost paper, but just to write the duet down again. His memory failed him, however, and he wound up writing a new piece to replace the fallen duet. Hidden within that story about physical laziness is a pearl about a man so talented and so befriended by time that he could toss off another piece of music without giving it a second thought. This is the same man who composed *The Barber of*

Seville in thirteen days because he had been too busy eating and drinking, and generally leading the high life during the months after receiving the commission for the opera.

And this is the man who penned the "Rice Aria." Notoriously late in finishing his scores, Rossini came in one day with his opera *Tancredi* still incomplete. "Have you put the rice up?" queried Rossini of his cook, for it was almost dinner time and, eschewing pasta, he had decided to have a *risotto* as a first course. Rossini sat down, and in the time it took to cook the rice, which Stendhal gives rather unbelievably as four minutes, Rossini composed what would become the most famous piece in the opera, "Di tanti palpiti," a cavatina for castrato, and the only part of *Tancredi* to have remained in the repertoire; it is now often sung as a concert piece by mezzos. The anecdote got around and "Di tanti palpiti" soon had the nickname of "Rice Aria" or "Rice Cavatina."[3]

From the beginning then—for Stendhal is writing this biography in 1824, at the height of Rossini's fame—Rossini times his music to food, dilates the time of writing so that he can toss off a duet in a mere quarter-hour, a cavatina in the time it takes to make rice, and an opera, considered by many to be his masterpiece, in less than two weeks. So, one wonders, what could Rossini do in the time it takes to make pasta. Produce an aria, a cavatina, or a duet? Steal his own overture, as he was wont to do? No, in fact, in the time it takes to make pasta, Rossini could do nothing more than make pasta. Even with the already prepared fresh or dried noodles at hand, pasta is all-consuming. Oh, perhaps a little side dish here and there, or a poor-man's dessert. Among Rossini's pieces written after *William Tell*, and collected in his *Sins of My Old Age*, one finds *Four Hors d'oeuvres*, entitled *Radishes, Anchovies, Pickles and Butter*, and *Four Beggars [Les Quatre Mendiants]*, the name of a dessert composed of figs, almonds, raisins, and hazelnuts, precisely the names Rossini gives these pieces. But nothing so glorious as "Di tanti palpiti" would be written while the noodles were cooking.

When Rossini abandoned the opera, he continued as writer, composer, and conductor, but in his own kitchen. He ate and ate and ate and this not being enough—for in so doing, he was merely performing what others had composed—he composed his own dishes. Three retain our interest, all bearing his name: the most famous, Tournedos Rossini, its lighter cousin, Eggs Rossini, and the most infamous, the most secret, and the most amazing of the three, Macaroni Rossini. The beef dish gets fair coverage in most culinary encyclopedias, including the *Larousse gastronomique*, Ali-Bab's *Gastronomie pratique*, and Escoffier's *Le Guide culinaire,* the egg dish is often mentioned as well, but not one of these three codifications of French cooking mentions Macaroni Rossini. The recipe for the tournedos is fairly straightforward, as Philippe Coudere gives it in his book *Les Plats qui on fait la France:* a tournedos (filet mignon), a slice or two of foie gras (fresh of course), butter, truffles, a crouton, and Madeira to deglaze the pan. Some versions make a Madeira sauce with a demi-glace, but that is perhaps gilding the lily. For the dish, Eggs Rossini, the eggs—sometimes poached as in Eggs Benedict, sometimes scrambled, and sometimes in an omelet—are mixed or garnished with lavish amounts of foie gras and truffles, Rossini's two mainstays in the kitchen.

But the macaroni are something else again. One nineteenth-century deipnosophist named Méry, who was a guest at Rossini's table, waxes poetic: "Burnished like gold, perfumed like the East, fluid like the ambrosia of Olympus, a macaroni of drinkable sunbeams that burst in the middle of the dinner like the overture to *Semiramide*."[4] A bit dithyrambic for a plate of noodles. What was it? No one seemed to know. It was a secret even more well-guarded than the secret that makes castrati sing so well. In his book on foie gras, Serventi lists the ingredients for the dish: "large macaroni, then called 'of Naples,' goose foie gras, truffles, cooked ham, yolk of an egg, cream, salt and pepper."[5] Coudere does not include the truffles or the ham; the first seems to be a natural ingredient that may be included or not, depending on the prodigality of the host; the latter seems an unfortunate adulteration. Coudere adds that the macaroni are tossed with butter, gruyère, and Parmesan.[6]

Why all the praise and the mystery? Quite simply, the foie gras was not visible. The meltingly succulent flavor was there alright but it was nowhere to be seen. Let us turn to Frédéric Vitoux who waspishly argues that the Rossini of music and the Rossini of the kitchen are very different: "In short, the Rossini we see is not the same as the Rossini we hear. The first gives his name to a tournedos by smearing it with foie gras, a culinary heresy moreover. The second writes *The Barber of Seville* in two weeks, which seems impossible and we do not see how it is done."[7] Whereas in the beef dish, the heresy is visible, in the macaroni dish, the sin is nowhere to be seen. Indeed, Vitoux is right in a way: seeing is all-important. Just as it is impossible to see how anyone could write such a comic masterpiece in a fortnight, it is impossible to see how Rossini made his pasta. He did not tip his hand and kept the kitchen door closed. One imagines his cook (who became his second wife) sworn to secrecy with a blood oath. What we see is the performance of a soloist who looks as if he is performing magic. It was, of course, typical nineteenth-century behavior. People heard Paganini and saw his hair-raising stunts, yet no one believed them. Toward mid-century Franz Liszt "invented" the solo piano recital, and had the nerve to turn the piano sideways so people could see his devilish performance, yet still not believe what they saw.

The secret was revealed only after Rossini's death and is record-ed by Pierre Lacam, whose name homonymously promises much, and by Couderc among others.[8] Rossini had a silver syringe made especially for him. He would make a forcemeat out of foie gras, some seasoning, an egg, and perhaps some butter and fill the syringe with that forcemeat. Having cooked the mac-aroni, which we assume to be roughly the size of ziti, the Italian word for bridegrooms, he would let them cool a bit. He would then inject each one individually with the forcemeat. When all this was accomplished, he would reheat them with some butter, and toss in the Gruyère (the French touch) and the Parmesan (the Italian touch). When the pasta was hot and the cheese was melted, he would serve the magical dish to his friends. The jeal-ously guarded secret was discovered only after his death and it is said that the famous silver syringe brought a high price at auc-tion.

Timing is everything. The same man who would scribble "Di tanti palpiti" in the time it took to make a risotto would literal-ly spend hours individually stuffing each pasta tube with foie gras, only to make the effort disappear. For no one could see it, no one could know. To tell that the foie gras was there would make it visible; it would indeed be heresy in more ways than one. Delicious, supernal product of an inhuman method of pro-duction, foie gras is almost mythical in its luxurious richness, ethereal in its melting deliquescence, ambrosial in its gustatory pleasure. Foie gras is the sound of the castrato, the testicle of the castrato transubstantiated into his voice, celestial, heady, other-worldly. Vitoux is almost right, although the word is not heresy, but "sacred." As Léo Moulin demonstrates, organ meats are sacred, compelling and taboo at once, and because of that are even ambiguous in their naming; some words are variously defined as referring to different organs and there are often uncertain etymologies, as if "language hesitated in defining these strange meals clearly."[9]

Between the testicles of the castrati and the liver of the goose, between the cutting of a boy to produce heavenly music and the force-feeding of a goose to produce blissful taste, it is but a small step, a scrambled difference, ultimately none at all. Rossini, master of timing—one must know when to castrate the boy, when to kill the goose—takes the silver syringe that combines the metal of the blade with the hollowness of the feeding tube, and carefully, painstakingly, patiently fills each hollow noodle with the burnished voice and the missing flesh.

It is a simple enough task to prepare Macaroni Rossini for your friends and family. No proportions are given, as no recipe exists. Put a compact disk of the "Overture" to *William Tell* on your stereo system. Put some water up to boil. When the water boils, put on "di Tanti Palpiti" and cook some Ziti al dente in the time it takes the mezzo, or preferably the castrato if one can be found, to sing the recitative and aria. Separately, with a mortar and pestle, carefully turn some fresh goose foie gras into a puree, *sempre legato*. Season with salt and pepper. Prepare a forcemeat of the foie gras, an egg to bind the mixture, and perhaps some butter or cream. If you wish, you may add some appoggiaturas of chopped truffle. With the aid of a silver syringe you have had specially made for you at great cost, inject each of the noodles with some of the forcemeat. Reheat the pasta in some butter on top of the stove and add some gruyère and Parmesan cheese. Put Cinderella's joyful air "Non più mesta" on the stereo. When the pasta is piping hot and the cheese is melted, bring the dish to the table with a flourish. Serve your guests *con brio*, but refuse to reveal the secret of the dish.

Notes

1. Michotte, Edmond. *La Visite de R. Wagner à Rossini (Paris 1860). Détails inédits et commentaires. (Avec Portraits)* (Paris: Librairie Fishbacher), 1906, pp. 43-44.

2. Stendhal. *Vie de Rossini*, ed. Pierre Brunel (Paris: Gallimard [Folio], 1992), pp. 433-34.

3. Stendhal. p.89; Coudere, Philippe, *Les Plats qui ont fait la France. De l'andouillette au vol-au-vent* (Paris: Julliard, 1995), p. 174.

4. Quoted in Coudere, p. 94

5. Serventi, Silvano. *La Grande Histoire du foie gras* (Paris: Flammarion, 1993), p. 104.

6. Coudere, pp. 93-94

7. Vitoux, Frédéric. *Gioacchino Rossini* (Paris: Seoul, 1986), p. 60.

8. Lacam, Pierre. *Le Memorial historique et geographique de la patisserie* (Paris: privately printed, c. 1900[?], p. 88; Coudere, loc. cit.

9. Moulin, Leo. "Les Abats et le sacré," in *L'Imaginaire des nourritures*, ed. Simone Vierne (Grenoble: Presses Universitaires de Grenoble), p. 135.

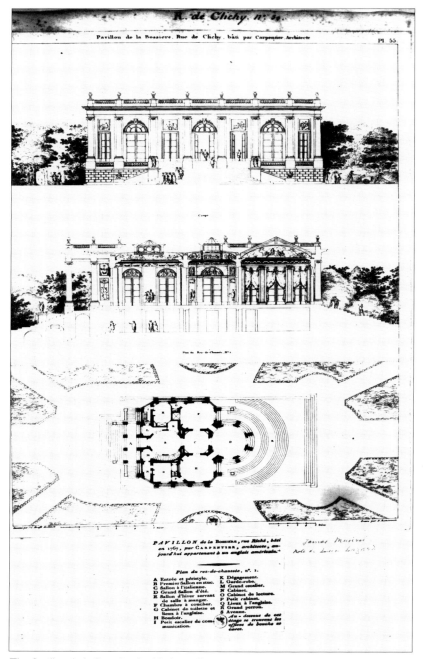

The *Pavillon de la Boissière,* by Mathieu Carpantier, elevation, section and plan drawings, 1751. This *maison de plaisance* in Clichy has most likely inspired Bastide's conception of the ideal *"petite maison."*

Rodolphe el-Khoury

Delectable Decoration:
Taste and Spectacle
in Jean François de Bastide's
La petite maison

Si j'ai du goût ce n'est guère
Que pour la terre et les pierres.

Arthur Rimbaud, "Fête de la faim"

Optic Taste/Haptic Desire

The first discussion at the Académie Royale de l'Architecture was launched in 1672 with the question: "What is good taste?" For the next century, architectural theorists sought practical and theoretical answers to this problem. The romantic movement eventually relegated the issue to the periphery of art, while it focused on invention and expression in the act of artistic creativity. The preoccupation with taste coincided initially with the pursuit of equilibrium and "justesse" in a culture of "honnêteté" and "bienséances" and was bound to become incompatible with the "great passions" of the romantic era. In the eighteenth century, however, the emancipation of taste from a doctrinal classicism and its reorientation toward an aesthetic of subjectivity allowed for Dionysian modes of engagement with beauty and the sublime and encouraged the meeting of the aesthetic and the erotic.

Architectural criticism in the seventeenth century tended to confine the sphere of taste to an aesthetic of "rules" based on the objectivity of a potentially quantifiable and analyzable language. As a faculty of critical discernment, taste tended to merge with judgment and came to designate the apprehension of rules as much as their application.[1] In the eighteenth-century, the mechanisms of taste were recast in psychological terms. Under the dominant influence of an English empiricist epistemology the sensuous categories of knowledge were rehabilitated: the apprehension of art became strictly aesthetic—i.e., sensuous—and its psychological mode was grounded in the "natural harmony" of the world.

Not only was taste identified with a natural faculty and more or less literally, with a sensory organ for the apprehension of the beautiful—"le sens interne du beau": "It is this sixth sense within us, whose organs we cannot see."[2] The purpose of aesthetic apprehension was also assigned to taste, "which is nothing other than to discover quickly and keenly the degree of pleasure that each thing should afford us." and was realigned with pleasure.[3]

In *Le Traité du Beau essentiel* (1742) Briseux accordingly theorizes the analogy of human and natural organizations to account for the psychological mechanisms of aesthetic pleasure:

> Since this universal mother [Nature] acts always with a single wisdom and in a uniform manner, we could rightfully conclude that the pleasures of seeing and hearing consist in the perception of harmonic relations as analogous to our constitution. This principle applies not only to music but to all the arts since the same cause could not have two different effects.[4]

The pleasure derived from the experience of the beautiful is thus due to a sympathetic rapport with the object of beauty; the intensity of the pleasure is furthermore calibrated to the resonance or intimacy of this sympathetic rapport:

> If proportions in music make a greater impression on the soul than do those in other objects of sensation, it is because music is more in sympathy with it, being more alive, as it were. So pronounced is this sympathy that we are more touched by a human voice than by the sound of instruments.[5]

When the object of beauty comes to life in the intimacy of aesthetic rapports, the pleasures of taste could equal the pleasures of love and the theory of taste coincides with the theory of love. The equation is most often noted in the case of gustative sensation. Gastronomy and eroticism have overlapped since the tasting of the forbidden fruit, but the oral proclivities of eros were particularly pronounced in the eighteenth century, when the libertine was typically known to match sexual excess with gastronomical indulgence.

Despite its undeniable occularcentrism, the aesthetic discourse of the Enlightenment repeatedly appealed to the mouth in order to demonstrate the immediacy and perspicacity of aesthetic apprehension: "We taste the stew, and even without knowing the rules governing its composition, we can tell whether it is good. The same holds true for painting and other products of the intellect that are intended to please us by touching us."[6] Voltaire's article "Goût" in the *Encyclopédie* also hinges on a rhetorical if not aphoristic comparison of "the ability to distinguish the tastes of our foods" and "a feeling for beauties and defects in all the arts."[7] He thus writes that taste:

> ...is like that of the tongue and the palate: a ready and unreflective discernment, sensitive and sensual in appreciating the good, violent in rejecting the bad, often lost and uncertain, not even knowing if it should be pleased by what is presented to it, and sometimes forming only by dint of habit.[8]

Voltaire's comparative argument eventually abandons the rhetorical symmetry of the simile to collapse the two parallel notions into "a kind of touch": "Taste is not content with seeing, with knowing the beauty of a work; it has to feel it, to be touched by it."[9]

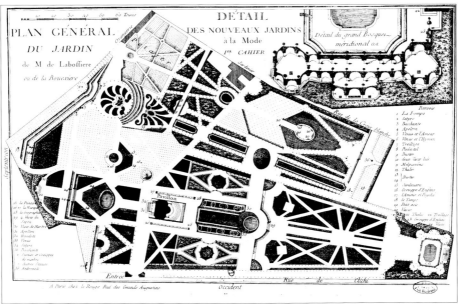

General Plan of M. de la Boissière's Garden.

Such comparisons were commonplace and consistently con-verged on the tactility of taste.[10] The gustative analog stressed the immediacy of apprehension in taste, the direct sensory con-tact with matter.[11] It projected a virtual tactility onto a visual mode of apprehension which operated at a distance from the object of its assimilating faculty. This distance—spatial and con-ceptual—is momentarily abolished in the virtual tactility of a latent (i.e. ideological) carnality. Thus implying haptic sensation in optic discernment, taste could naturalize and describe its aes-thetic assimilation in a kind of tactile vision, combining the immediacy of touch with the distance of sight.

Architecture in the Bedroom

The literature of the eighteenth century provides many instances where the semantic polyvalence and epistemological (ideological) indeterminacy of taste has a structuring role in the narrative and the device is most vividly illustrated in Jean-François de Bastide's *La Petite Maison*.[12] This novella narrates a plot of seduction involving a host, a guest, and a building. Trémicour, the host, is *an extraordinary man, a man of wit and taste*. Mélite, the guest, *had yet to take a lover; time that other women squandered in love and deception, Mélite spent in instruction, acquiring true taste and knowledge*. Trémicours challenged Mélite to visit his "petite maison" after she had frus-trated his otherwise irresistible advances: *they called a wager and there she went*. The calculated procession through the house, alternating interior and exterior spaces of shifting illu-sions and delicious luxuries structures the progress of the cou-ple through the various stages of the seduction.

The most remarkable aspect of the house is the "proto-function-alist" adaptation of the decoration to the specific purpose of each room. This architectural feature is emphasized in the structure of the narrative: a series of episodes with highly differ-entiated and precisely described settings; Mélite savors their dis-tinct "tastes" with increasing pleasure and abandon, propelling the plot with her incremental loss of inhibition.

The notion that architecture could inspire lustful designs is totally foreign today; the tendency is to trivialize it as a fanciful narrative twist that was concocted for the mere amusement of eighteenth-century readers, to dismiss it as a literary device that has little pertinence in historical analysis. The anecdotal or rhetorical inflation is unmistakable in Mélite's infatuation with

architecture; yet hyperbole is most effective when grounded—
however tenuously—in reality. An investigation of the text in
relation to eighteenth-century culture might thus reveal the
extent to which this allegory is in tune with actual aesthetic atti-
tudes, beliefs and modes of reception.

The key to this investigation is the notion of taste, considered in
its inherent ambiguities and historical vicissitudes. Bastide's use
of the term "goût" often overlaps with "caractère"—a term
shared with natural scientists such as Linnaeus, Buffon, and
Adanson, whose taxonomical procedures relied upon the identi-
fication of "general and particular characters." The terms *goût,
génie,* and *caractère* do tend to overlap and are often inter-
changeable in eighteenth-century texts. At the risk of oversim-
plification, one might distinguish their semantic spheres by sit-
uating them along the different stages of the cycle of production
and consumption. Taste is accordingly a fundamental precondi-
tion of genius; character is the imprint or mark left by genius in
the work; taste, again, is the receptive faculty which can discern
character. Taste hence encapsulates the system; it is a condition
of both production and reception. As a pivotal element in
Bastide's text, it reconciles the quality of the object with the
mode of its reception: the decoration in good taste is savored by
people of good taste. It is instrumental to the intimacy which
takes hold between the three protagonists, primarily in its ten-
dency to oscillate between incarnate sensory perception and
disembodied intellectual discernment, the capacity, in short, to
blur the distinction between the beautiful, the desirable, and the
edible.

In the climactic scene, Mélite, deceptively led into a second
boudoir, collapses into a *bergère,* to assume her designated role
among the *marquises, duchesses,* and *otomanes*— other objects
furnishing the boudoir: *The threat was terrible, the situation
even more so. Mélite shuddered, faltered, sighed, and lost the
wager.* The narrative thus concludes with the imminent execu-
tion of the deferred act while the last word cynically switches
the tone of the climaxing narrative to the bare "economics" of
the sexual transaction.

This second boudoir, the ultimate destination for the concluding
seduction is described as follows:

> This new room, next to which lay a wardrobe, was
> stretched with thick green gourgouran. The most beau-
> tiful engravings by Cochin, Lebas, and Cars were hung

symmetrically on the walls. The room was lit just enough to allow the masterpieces of these skillful masters to be seen.

In comparison to the gilded, mirrored and lavishly decorated rooms of the house, the boudoir stands out in its sobriety. The author/architect has even taken the care to substitute the severe lines of presumably monochromatic engravings for the ethereal rococo paintings found elsewhere. Lighting is one of the few mentioned features, it is designed to favor the engraved contours. Everywhere else, lighting is spectacular: it is meant to enchant, dazzle and deceive . The contrast is sharpest in the first boudoir where light is cast in a characteristically theatrical mode:

> The walls of the boudoir were covered with mirrors whose joinery was concealed by carefully sculpted, leafy tree trunks. The trees, arranged to give the illusion of a quincunx, were heavy with flowers and laden with chandeliers. The light from their many candles receded into the opposite mirrors, which had been purposely veiled with hanging gauze. So magical was this optical effect that the boudoir could have been mistaken for a natural woods, lit with the help of art.

None of the optical devices and illusions of the erotic theater are tolerated in the austere light of the museum-like boudoir, yet it is deliberately chosen as the setting for the *denouement* of the sexual battle. Indeed, Trémicour decisively led Mélite into the second boudoir and *stepped on her dress when she was at the threshold, so that in turning her head to disengage her dress, she would not see the place she was entering.* One wonders why he took this precaution. Why should he avert Mélite's gaze from a seemingly inoffensive decor when her delicate sensibility had braved more sensually composed effects? And why should this sober room, and not any other, occupy this privileged position at the conclusion of an erotically charged itinerary?

No particular features could indeed characterize the room as a boudoir except for the furniture. Unlike other spaces in the house where signs of sensuality are encrypted in the decoration, the erotic is here delivered literally, i.e., in functional pieces of equipment. Without Trémicour's deceptive intervention, Mélite would certainly have avoided a distasteful room, distasteful in the explicit destination of its furnishings and especially in its blandness, i.e., *in its lack of taste.* The second boudoir is most

Still Life Showing Gold and Silver Pieces from the Royal Collection, by Alexandre-François Desportes. A composition of fruit, meat and silverware characteristic of the ostentatious culinary spectacles in the reign of Louis XIV.

threatening to Mélite because it offers no objects to her taste. In the second boudoir, she is left alone with Trémicour and no other channels for the sublimation of her libidinal appetite in aesthetic assimilation.

In the second boudoir, architecture provides a support, a functional decor for an action unfolding separately in the foreground; in the garden, in all the other rooms and especially in the first boudoir, architecture participated in the action. Not only was it a catalyst that provided the optimal ambiance and the necessary lubricant for the machinations of seduction, it also engaged the protagonists as the subject of a sublimated amorous rapport. We may say that architecture, in La Petite Maison, performs the role of a sexual partner—that is, with the exception of the second boudoir, where Trémicour could more effectively deal his last card, in the absence of his rival and accomplice.

Architecture in the Dining Room

Let us backtrack to another critical episode in the narrative: the scene in the dining room, where our protagonist are involved in a more literal mode of consumption. In a narrative organized

Design for table-top decoration using powdered sugar (sablage) in the imitation of a garden parterre from Gillier's *Le Cannaméliste français*, 1758.

around taste and vision, or more precisely, around the *taste of vision,* the supper scene, the moment where taste literally switches to a haptic mode, should prove significant.

No mention of actual food is made in *La Petite Maison's* culinary scene; we merely learn that Mélite *ate little and wanted to drink only water.* During the brief meal where only tasteless water is specified, her attitude displays no signs of the alert and inquisitive concentration of the gourmet; she was rather distracted, Her mood introspective, detached: *she was more preoccupied with her anguish than with the things that had caused it.* As Mélite's body engages in a most tactile activity, her mind disconnects from the external objects of sensory assimilation to withdraw into an idealizing interiority. The sensuous experience of matter in eating does not interfere with the reflecting consciousness which remains indifferent to its taste. In *La Petite Maison,* food is indeed tasteful as long as it is assimilated into decoration and consumed as spectacle.

In the dining room, *where a table was laid out with an elaborate meal,* no servants are in sight and no service is mentioned. We are thus to assume that the meal in question is a "repas en ambigu." The type was in fashion since the late-seventeenth century and consists of a simultaneous presentation of more or less contrasting dishes in lieu of the usual consecutive courses. In *L'Art de bien traiter* (1674)—milestone of a growing culinary literature, the "ambigu" is defined in the following passage:

> This manner of serving is strictly speaking, the combination of a supper and a light meal and is generally served at day's end; and instead of dividing a meal into several courses, all is set out together from the start, but arranged and ordered in a highly specific way that is agreeable and pleasurable to the senses and that brings appetite even to the most fastidious.[13]

The "ambigu" is distinguished primarily by its spatial organization. It rivals a "souper" or a "collation," not necessarily in the constitution and taste of individual dishes, but rather in the potential for elaborate formal compositions. Indeed, in instances of particular luxury the *ambigu* could transform the whole dining room into a culinary theater, "for aside from the ordinary meats that are set out on tables, sweets, wines and lights are everywhere visible in the banquet room, on cabinets, on fireplace mantles, and in other more convenient locations where they are so immaculately displayed that there is no image, painting, spectacle, or ornament, however rich and orderly, that might compare to them."[14]

In the "ambigu", the temporal succession of multiple courses is thus eliminated in favor of the visual effect of a unified tableau. Such meals are composed as a spectacle for the eyes and do not necessarily involve an oral consumption of food: "the pleasure of seeing them is greater than that of touching them" states L. S. R. They are modeled after painting, sculpture, and architecture and conform to their "rules" of visual composition. Grimod de la Reynière would thus praise a Duffoy, "the most dexterous decorator in Paris in terms of the dessert *surtout*," for the architectural orthodoxy of his culinary constructions: "We have admired the majestic scope of his temples and his palaces, wherein all the laws of architecture are perfectly observed; platters constructed with the highest elegance and in the most excellent taste."[15] The "surtout de table", the central element of the "ambigu", is often directly transposed from the stage set of the theater and is evidently not meant for oral consumption. One particularly elaborate model is again described in Grimod's *Almanach des gourmands*:

> This surtout or rather this reclining scape..., was three feet long, twenty inches wide and thirty high. It displayed the two principal stages of the *Opéra des Bardes*; behold the dream scene on one side and the recognition scene between Rosmala and her father on the other, and in the cavities of the rock that graced the center of the decoration were nestled several other scenes, ·among these that of the bridge.[16]

Carême, celebrity-cook and architecte manqué, later took a particular interest in the architectural potentials of pastry and devoted many copiously illustrated volumes to this art. They demonstrated designs in different styles and with considerable attention to decoration and proportion. The "pâte fine" allowed for minute details and great precision in execution while the traditional "pâte d'office" provided the primary building material for this edible architecture. Here is Carême's recipe:

Pâte d'Office (Office or Confectioner's Dough)

> This is of the utmost use in modern pastry. Sift one pound and a half of flour, make a hollow in it, and put in two eggs and three yolks, on a pound of pounded sugar, and a little salt; stir these for two minutes, that the sugar may be somewhat melted, then work in the flour, and if

Designs for edible architecture from Antoine Carême, *Le Pâtissier national parisien*, 1815.

necessary, another yolk, so as to render it as firm as if
for building a pie; fold it five or six time; it ought to be
smooth and well blended, otherwise add another yolk or
white of egg: afterwards cut the paste in pieces, mould
and roll it for the thickness of an inch, to serve for the
bottoms (or boards) of a "pièce montée"; put the paste
on a baking sheet slightly buttered, and with the fingers
press out the air between the paste and the sheet (with-
out this precaution the heat would deform it, and from
the heat not acting equally throughout, it would possess
less solidity); when thus arranged, cut it with the point
of a knife, as may be wished, and prick it to assist the
escape of the air; wash the surface slightly, but not the
sides, put it into a moderate oven, and if it blisters, pass
the blade of a large knife under it (if done enough) turn
it over to obtain a light brown color on both sides; when
taken from the oven lay it on the most even part of the
dresser, and place the baking-sheet upon it to remain
until cold, when the paste will be perfectly level on both
sides. All boards of "Pâte d'office" are thus made.[17]

In the scopic regime of this culinary "appareil", the haptic char-
acter of food is entirely undermined: to *eat* an "ambigu", to *taste*

it, is to *consume a spectacle* modeled after painting, decoration, and architecture, laid out in a particular formal style and with *bon goût*. The "repas en ambigu" is thoroughly theatrical; "it is a one-act play," writes Philip Stewart, "it seeks the utmost impact in the first glance; it attempts to embrace the entire range of possibilities in a single scene."[18] L. S. R. provides specific staging instructions for this culinary ensemble in his treatise; the glittering "appareil" of the Baroque theater is no doubt the prime source of inspiration:

> A confusion of lights should fill the room; use mirrored panels and other carefully imagined flourishes to form a glorious device that offers a pleasurable spectacle to the guests and unleashes joy by its charming diversity.[19]

In the *blinding light* of the petite maison's dining room, the baroque drama peaked when the theatrical machinery was set in motion, when the table flew down into the basement kitchen while another one rushed down from the upper floor to fill the gap left by the vanished meal.[20] This coup-de-théâtre, worthy of the new Salle des Machines at the Tuileries, pulled Mélite out of her momentary rêverie: *This feat, incredible to Mélite, roused her from self-absorption and invited her to consider anew the beauty and the ornamentation of the place that was offered for her admiration.*

The meal that Mélite barely touches thus participates in the decorative program of the dining room; it is designed to suggest an "avant-goût" of the ornamental delicacies on the wall depicting *the pleasures of the table and the pleasures of love.*

La Petite Maison's supper stages a scene of transubstantiation: stone comes alive for the cannibalizing gaze of an excited *goût*, while food is petrified into an architecture of *the highest elegance and in the best of taste.* In Bastide's dining room, food, the object of haptic assimilation, does not escape the tyranny of the scopic regime. Its haptic character is dissolved in a theatrical presentation which mobilize the senses for a scenography of flying tables and *blinding six stemmed candelabra.* Non-visual modes of assimilation and other senses are of course involved in the experience of the petite maison; they however conform to the logic of the spectacle and do not challenge the supremacy of sight—the privileged perceptual apparatus in the projection of desire. In Trémicour's petite maison, the scents of violet, jasmine, and rose are wondrously perceived—they are released from the varnish of woodwork—and music is magically heard at a sign from the host—it is performed by musicians hidden behind a partition. In both cases, the cause or source of sensation is inaccessible and incomprehensible to the spectator. The senses are disoriented and the feeling is one of wonder and bewilderment: in *La Petite Maison*, the pleasures of scents and music are diffused and intoxicating, they belong to the total dazzlement of the spectacle.

Food is equally spectacular; after it had performed as an appetizing figurant in the mise-en-scene of sublimated desires, it is promptly withdrawn from the scene so as not to interfere with the taste of the pièce de résistance. As an omnivorous gaze begins to savor the decoration, to lick and fondle its delicate carvings, penetrate the perspectival cavities of its pictorial representations, the meal—material evidence and reminder of a genuinely haptic experience—is dramatically rushed down into the coulisses, with the help of the baroque machinery that might have snatched a Don Juan, through a trap-door in the stage, from the "festin de pierre."

Notes:
1. See Françoise Fichet, *La Théorie architecturale à l'age classique*, Bruxelles, 1979, p. 36.
2. Jean-Batiste Du Bos, *Réfléxions critiques sur la peinture et sur la poësie*, Paris 1719, vol II, p. 342; reprint, Genève, 1967, p. 225.
3. Montesquieu, "Goût," in Denis Diderot and Jean le Rond d'Alembert, *Encyclopédie ou dictionnaire raisonné des sciences, des arts et des métiers, par une société des gens de lettres*, M. Neufchastel, 1751-1777, p. 762.
4. Charles Étienne Briseux, *Traité du Beau essentiel*, Paris, 1742, p. 45
5. Ibid, p. 47
6. Jean-Batiste Du Bos, *Réfléxions critiques*, reprint, p. 225, (emphasis added).
7. François Marie Arouet de Voltaire, "Goût," in Denis Diderot and Jean le Rond d'Alembert, *Encyclopédie*, p. 761.
8. Ibid.
9. Ibid.
10. Etymologically, the tactility of "taste" is more evident than "goût." It is related to the French "tâter" and features "touch, grope, feel, explore by touch, to have carnal knowledge of..." as immediate antecedents to "perceive by the sense of taste." (Oxford English Dictionary)
11. "Taste is not content with seeing, with knowing the beauty of a work; it has to feel it, to be touched by it." Voltaire, "Goût," in Denis Diderot and Jean le Rond d'Alembert, *Encyclopédie*, p. 761.
12. Jean François de Bastide, "La Petite Maison," in *Le Nouveau spectateur*, 1758, no. 2, pp. 361-412. Republished in Contes, in 3 vols.,

Paris, 1763, vol. II, pp. 47-88. The passages in italic are quoted from *The Little House; an Architectural Seduction*, New York: Princeton Architectural Press, 1996, a translation by Rodolphe el-Khoury, that is based on the 19th-century edition, *La Petite Maison*, Paris, 1879.

J. F. de Bastide (1724-98), a prolific writer who had gained some notoriety in the eighteenth century (Madame de Pompadour was one of his readers), was mostly appreciated for novels and plays dealing with *l'amour galant: La trentaine de cythère, Le Tribunal de l'amour ou les causes célèbres de cythère, Les Ressources de l'amour, Les Graduations de l'amour*, etc.

13. L. S. R., *L'Art de bien traiter*, Paris, 1674, pp. 359-60.

14. Ibid, pp. 372-73.

15. Grimod de la Reynière, *Almanach des Gourmands*, Paris, 1808, p. 227.

16. Ibid, p. 71.

17. Marie Antonin Carême, French cookery comprising *L'art de la cuisine française, Le pâtissier royal, Le cuisinier parisien*, translated by William Hall, London: J. Murray, 1836, p. 143.

18. As noted by Philip Stewart, the relation between the "ambigu" and the theater extends beyond the analogy with spectacle. In the late seventeenth century, the "repas en ambigu" lends its name to a series of plays and in 1769, to a theater specializing in the genre: *L'Ambigu Comique* on the boulevard du Temple. The title of Montfleury's play of 1673 *L'Ambigu comique ou les amours de Didon et d'Enée, tragédie en 3 actes, mêlée de trois intermèdes comiques*, is particularly evocative in its culinary inspiration: "the play is much like a course that alternates flesh with sweets." Philip Stewart, *Literature et gastronomie*, p. 89.

19. L. S. R., *L'Art de bien traiter*, p. 74.

20. "Tables volantes" ("flying tables') or "tables machinées" were built for royal residences such as Bellevue and Choisy by Guerin. One was also projected by Loriot for the Petit Trianon but was never built. One of its multiple versions is described in the *Mercure de France*:

> This table is composed of a fixed frame and of four side platforms. The whole is lifted all at once by a machine in such a way that the surface of the table, the frame as well as its attachments, is composed by a section of the raised floor... When the guests enter the dining room, there is not the least sign of a table; all that can be seen is a uniform floor that is adorned by a rose at its center. At the slightest nod, the leaves are retracted under the floor, and a table laden with food makes its sudden ascent, flanked by four servants emerging through the four openings. (Quoted in Jean-Claude Bonnet, *Écrits gastronomiques*, Paris, 1978, pp. 64-65.)

Daniel Spoerri

La Faim du C.N.A.C.

Dîner de la Société Homonyme

(Excerpts)

5. thus the recipe of Ali Bab, thus Alexandre Babinski, thus his brother Joseph, thus the syndrome and its sign; the alteration of the plantar reflex, but also the gold of the Celts, thus Yves Klein (born 1928, died 1962), thus his paintings of gold leaf, thus his zones of immaterial sensibility exchanged for gold bars, thus, as Hains says, "Arman's garbage pails that are exchanged for gold." See 15 and 47.

17. Thus Olivier Mosset (born in 1944 in Neuchâtel) and his O and his rounds, thus *The Story of O* of Pauline Réage, thus *The Marquise d'O* of Heinrich von Kleist, thus the olives ordered in the restaurant Sous l'Olivier (Under the Olive Tree) where I had lunch with Daniel Abadie on March 5th, the feast day of Sainte Olive, thus Oliveta, as Dali called Gala—see 107—because of the perfect oval of her face, but let's return to the round slices of onions, thus the onion watches of Claude Lalanne—see 85— thus Dali's soft watches, which he called *The Persistence of Memory*, thus, why not, my garret on the rue de l'Étoile—see 1— where I prepared to become a star-dancer, and which I reconstruct, by memory, in Tinguely's *The Head*. See 62.

28. Thus the poached eggs that I would have preserved with Ono, a chemical used to preserve eggs, thus Yoko Ono, the wife of John Lennon and his Plastic Ono Band, their record *I Imagine John Lennon*, thus Fluxus, its founder Georges Maciunus and George Brecht, Robert Filliou, Ben, Dick Higgins, Emmet Williams and me; but also, more directly, Roland Topor, thus his check for a million where the six zeros—see 26—are six farts (pets) let out by a man bent over like the number 1, thus his

Dîner

de la

Société Homonyme

POTAGES

Consommé Brieux 1 aux lettres 2
Potage de queues de kangourou Lacroix 3
Soupe albigeoise Heinz 4
Consommé aux pailleten d'or 5

ENTRÉES FROIDES

Saucisson d'âne 6
Rosette de Lyon Lhoste 7 et saucisson de Lion 8
Petit et grand Jésus 9
Rotwurst 10
Corned beef Minko 11
Sardines Pascal 12 au beurre Gauthier 13
Sardines Robert 14
Sardines d'argent à l'huile d'or 15
Sardines Parmentier 16 aux olives et rondelles d'oignons 17
Sardines Falstaff 18 à la sauce Tosca 19
Harengs marinés Dansk Pop 20
Maquereaux au naturel Geisha 21
Caviar pressé du Pontus-Euxinus 22
Schiller 23 Locken

Salade de coquilles saint Jacques 24 à la manière du chef Meunière 25

ENTRÉES CHAUDES

Quenelles de saumon Mack 26 à la sauce Nantua Giraudet 27
œufs pochés Roland 28

POISSON

Raie 29 Roger Nellens 30 au vinaigre de notre mère 31

ENTRÉES D'ABATS ET VIANDES

Tripes Pharamond 32 à la mode de Caen 33
Jambon à l'ananas 34, riz Uncle Ben's 35 au sel Brecht's 36 ou Choucroute Christ 37
Chateaubriands 38 servis bleu 39 des boucheries Bacon 40, Delaunay 41, Léger 42, E. Martin 43, St André Morin 44,
Rousseau 45 et Schwartz 46, garniture Pommes de terre Pommes 47 rabotées 48 sautées au four, vierbe la gras

Flageolets Gravier **51**

Mon de veau à la bourgaise des boucheries Raymond et Roussel **52**

Andouillette Yves le Pape **53** et sa purée bretonne au caof **54**

Lion ce Claude **55**

SALADE

Romaine à l'Olio Dante **56** et à la moutarde de Meaux **57**

FROMAGES AU BEURRE D'ÉCHIRÉ **58**

Roquefort Société **59**
Carré Ministre **60**
Demi-Pont-Lévêque **61**
Le petit Jeannot **62**
Emmenthal **63**
Fromage Le Merle **64**
Le petit Descartes **65**
Camembert Claudel **66**
Le petit Briennois **67**

DESSERTS

Poires Williams **68** aux gâteaux Kossuth **69**
Confitures Hero **70** avec langues de chat **71** et palets Cadiou **72**
Confitures de pommes Pollaiolo **73**
Oranges Pigalle **74** et Palermo **75**
Mont Blanc **76** à la crème de marron Santa Rosa **77**
Far breton **78** , éclairs **79** , Paris-Brest **80**
Conversations **81**

Griottes au sirop Vitrac **82** avec biscuits Garibaldi **83** de Jacob's **84**
Reines Claudes **85** au sirop et biscuits de Reims **86**
Pruneaux d'Agen **87** Fernand Point **88**
Biber de la confiserie Spörri **89**
Glaces Fisher **90**

Leibnitz **91** Keks, biscuits Adam **92** et sablés de Retz **93**

Brioches **94** aux oreillons de Paris **95**

La Pirrade **96** de Nôtre **97**

Café torréfié **98** au lait cru **99** de la Selle sur le Bied **100**
Sucre St Louis pure canne **101**
Infusions Pagès **102**,

Pensée sauvage **103**

Mémoires d'un vieux con, thus the movement Panique, but also Roland Penrose at whose place I danced an entire night with Françoise Gilot, thus Roland Pen*rose* Sélavy, thus the pen name of Marcel Duchamp, thus his spoonerisms (contrepètries): *Lits et ratures, Fresh Widow* or *L.H.O.O.Q.* See 77.

29. Thus Man Ray (born 1890) thus the rayographs, thus the author of the *Trompe-l'Oeuf*, thus the Surrealist Holy Trinity: eye, egg, testicle—see 127—thus my *détrompe-l'oeil*, thus his "Cadeau," thus his metronome that I published in the first edition of MAT *(Multiplication d'Art Transformable)* in 1959.

33. Thus à la mode de Lacan, according to Hains, thus Jacques Lacan, in-law of Georges Bataille, thus *Story of the Eye* to return to nos. 28 and 29, thus the École Freudienne with a sauce of the raw and the cooked, but also the idea of a visceral auto-cannibalism: a stomach that digests a stomach, which is at the core of my collection of at least 400 recipes for tripe, thus Robert Morel—see 120—who still awaits the manuscript.

64. Le Merle goat's-milk cheese produced by D. Cochon, thus quite a task, to be added to the fantastic bestiaries of Borges and Christian Morgenstern, thus another homonymous travesty of a dinner that could be made with bread from the bakeries of Leveau (Veal), Fauve (Wild Animal), Boudin (Sausage), Poisson (Fish), Jarret (Knuckle), Goujon (Gudgeon), and steaks from the butchers: Petit (Little), Pain (Bread), Poisson (Fish), Leloup (The Wolf), Millet, Lion, Collin (Hake), and Gâteau (Cake), to cite just a few to be found in the Loiret.

97. Thus the pastry chef Gaston Lenôtre and his book *La pâtisserie selon Lenôtre,* thus André Le Nôtre (1613-1700), thus the creator of the jardin à la française, thus the gardens of Vaux-le-Vicomte and of Versailles, thus Julio Le Parc, a noble ancestry that he certainly didn't suspect until now.

157. Thus Robert Malaval (born 1937), creator in 1961 of the *Aliment Blanc* (White Foodstuff), the recipe or formula of which he now refuses to divulge, thus the sentence of Otto Hahn in L'Express: "For Malaval, the act of painting is accompanied by no theoretical considerations, but it is nevertheless his intelligence that directs the game."

164. Thus the sentence of Robert Desnos written in 1922: "Aux agapes de Rrose Sélavy on mange du pâté de Pape dans une sauce couleur d'agate" (During Rrose Sélavy's feasts one eats pâté of Pope with an agate-colored sauce."

George H. Bauer

Regendering the Fig

But what of fruits, Nathaniel what of fruits?

André Gide, Fruits of the Earth

ruit salad, Bruce Rodgers explains in his *Gay Talk*,[2] is a "large gathering of homosexuals; a gay crowd or audience." A fruit predilection seemed to flourish in the thirties and included every variety, but Rodgers does single out the banana as a synonym. For my own reasons, figs were what I was looking for, but alas in leafing through his dictionary I find only "Fig: (rare) posing strap." Fruit and banana are both nouns and adjective: "That banana acts as if he were five going on four." or "Loving you has made me bananas." The fare is rich from fruitsy, fruity, the athletic fruit bowl queen to fruit baskets and fruitbars (Fig Newtons of my imagination remained eccentric, odd but not really gay). *The Random House Historical Dictionary of American Slang* concludes its gay fruit cornucopia with M. Korda writing in the New Yorker on March 29, 1993: "Surely nobody had used the word 'fruit' to describe a homosexual since the thirties."[3]

"My salad days,/ When I was green in judgment," as Liz Taylor aka Cleopatra opined, certainly characterized my innocence growing up in the thirties and forties. Greens were there for hot, wilted lettuce or an excuse for a combination salad where the lettuce was buried under sliced cucumbers, ripe olives, diced celery, shredded green peppers, and quarters of bright red tomatoes. Salad meant fruit salad. In my Mother's and Grandmother's kitchen I learned the art of the fruit salad. Fruit in every combination, gay in color, and in the presentation and naming I found pure art and poetry. As powerfully evocative for me in image and taste as Proust's own madeleines dipped in tisane for the young

narrator, this Candlestick Salad never fails to release a flood of memories. The receipt (recipe if you prefer) is simple. Take a firm banana six inches in length, gently peel it. Slice an inch off its bottom so it will stand on its own. On a bed of lettuce place a slice of chilled pineapple and insert the banana upright in the hole. Dribble a little mayonnaise (Miracle Whip, if you like) on the tip and sides and top with a bright red maraschino cherry piece. Sprinkle lightly with grated cheese or coconut flakes according to your taste. Without Freud, without slang, how would I know the banana was so sexy and quite simply a penis in the vernacular: "I have a girl in Indiana/She liked to play with my banana."[4] Random randily apprises me that to get one's banana peeled was "to engage in copulation—And thus the tawdry hussy his ripe banana peeled." The candlestick salad was innocence itself. "He's bananas, he's sexually perverted, a degenerate;" "a queer."[5] Out of the question.

Bananas were for salad. Life was just a bottle of maraschino cherries. The sexiest, most tantalizing connection with the world of seduction by fruit was a youthful passion for the Brazilian Bombshell known as "The Divine Carmen Miranda." She was a living, singing embodiment of a fruit goddess.[6] I never missed one of her films. *Weekend in Havana*, *That Night in Rio*—watching her do her Latin numbers on incredible six to ten inch platform shoes dripping in exotic and erotic fruit all topped by a heady combination of every fruit imaginable atop her five foot two inches. A couple of songwriters wrote a "Carmen Banana" number for her. She rejected it and it became the "Chiquita Banana" song of the United Fruit company. *In Babes on Broadway* of 1942, a top banana himself, Mickey Rooney, borrowed the whole bowl of fruit and gave us a different meaning to her tunes. In full fig. Figged out. In fioc'chi.

The male gender of the banana in all its applications seems never to have been in doubt. Christians never conceive of it as "the fruit of paradise" or *musa paradisia* on the Roman tongue. Robert Hendrickson in his *Foods for Love*[7] tells us that "both the Moslems and Romans of later times believed that the plantain or cooking banana was the forbidden fruit in the Garden of Eden" before noting that "Arabian Slang and a score more languages make the fruit a symbol for the male organ, and 'I had a banana with Lady Diana' as English slang for intercourse from the beginning of the century up until about 1930."[8] The case of the fig is more difficult and all the more interesting to me in its absence from my youthful cooking lessons and recipes. The fig leaf, however, was ever present hiding, puritanically, something in Garden and Kitchen. The original apron. Eating the fruit was an eye-opener. "And the eyes of them both were opened, and they knew that they were naked; and they sewed fig leaves together, and made themselves aprons."[9] From this patched up attire, hardly full fig, the ambiguity begins. In *The Erotic Tongue*, Lawrence Paros sheds a little light. "Since Adam and Eve both reputedly covered their nakedness with a fig leaf, the fig has come to be identified with the *vagina*, the *penis* and even the act itself. The appearance of the split fig added further to the case because it so closely resembles the lips [the labia] of the vulva."[10] Even the Greeks saw both sides of this succulent fruit. "A common source of double entendres for the organs of both sexes is the fig, although such references to the female member far outnumber references to the male member."[11] In *The Peace* (421 B.C.) Aristophanes evokes a paradise of figs. "Now live splendidly together./Free from adversity./Pick figs./May his be large and hard,/May hers be sweet."

Any hint of maleness is gone by the late 1980s when Alan Richter offers up his treaties on *The Language of Sexuality*.[12] There fig is simply glossed: female genitals. For the etiquette of eating such a morsel, D.H. Lawrence is not just an authoritative specialist of gardens and gardeners. But in his poem *Figs* he lays down the law for well-mannered fig eating.

> The proper way to eat a fig, in society,
> Is to split it in four, holding it by the stump,
> And open it, so that it is a glittering, rosy, moist, honied, heavy-petalled four-petalled flower.

> Then you throw away the skin
> Which is just like a four-sepalled calyx,
> After you have taken off the blossom with your lips.
>
> But the vulgar way
> Is just to put your mouth in the crack, and take out the flesh
>   in one bite.

But the creator of Lady Chatterley and her lover in gardens Edenic wants to be sure his cunning not be mistook for fellatio.

> The fig is a very secretive fruit.
> As you see it standing, growing, you feel at once it is symbolic:
> And it seems male.
> But when you come to know it better, you agree with the
>   Romans, it is female.

As if to definitively erase any taste of maleness, his lyricism seeks new heights rising from the Latin to Vulgar Latin to his own native tongue.

> The Italians vulgarly say, it stands for the female part; the
>   fig-fruit:
> The fissure, the yoni,
> The wonderful moist conductivity towards the centre.
>   . . .
> Folded upon itself, and secret unutterable,
> And milky-sapped, sap that curdles milk and makes *ricotta*,
> Sap that smells strange on your fingers, that even goats won't
>   taste it.[13]

Clearly his fig is no mere trifle, but the "fruit of the female mystery." The woman-fig/fig-woman comes into culinary picture where the eating of the fig turns into a terrible punishment. "To fig" takes on a new flavor to become the worst of insults, the *fico*. This obscene gesture of disdain or contempt is made by placing the thumb between the first and second fingers. Its power is mystifying without the help of the encyclopedic knowledge of the fig found in the *Nouveau Larousse Illustré*.[14] "Faire la figue à tous ses ennemis" shares with us this anecdote that has been used to explain this different twist on fig eating. "The good citizens of Milan, having revolted against the Emperor Frederick Barbarossa (Red Beard), had ignominiously run his wife the Empress out of town seated ass-backward on an old mule named Tacor. Frederick, having subjugated them, wanted to inflict a striking vengeance: he had a *fig* stuck up the ass of his mule, and all the Milanese prisoners were forced to use their teeth to remove this fig in public or be hanged and strangled on the spot." Just desserts.

Lawrence's appreciation for the fig is almost purist in nature. Surprisingly his considered expertise with figs does not find it's way into Alex Comfort's *The Joy of Sex: A Gourmet Guide to Love Making*.[15] For fruits in combination with variations of gourmandism around the secretive fig, let me dip into Gershon Legman's *Ora-genitalism: Oral Techniques in Genital Excitement*[16] for some directions that will never find their way into *The Joy of Cooking*.[17] "Sophisticates often insert into the vagina fruits such as strawberries or cherries (sweet, pitted cherries), or sections of an orange (a seedless orange), or slices of apple deliciously dipped in honey; thereupon sucking or drawing them out of the vagina again, and eating them with relish (sic).

The classical fruit used in this way is the banana, which is (with the serpent) the oldest and most famous of all phallic symbols, and one of the commonest objects used by women as a natural dildo, as are cucumbers and carrots."[18] Leaving aside the vegetables, he concentrates on the *musa paradisia* avoiding the fig and the asp covered by fig leaves. I have already noted the Moslem and Roman propensity to insert the banana in the story of Adam and Eve. Legman reaffirms the banana temptation. "According to Mohammedan legend, the fruit of Eden with which Eve sinned was a banana—the large red banana of the tropics, is meant—since the Bible does not specify anywhere that Eve used an apple: 'the fruit of the tree' says *Genesis*, 3;1-7, without details. I have been told that it is possible for a woman with good muscle-tone in her vagina to peel back a ripe banana a short distance, to insert the peeled tip into her vagina, and to peel and draw in all the rest of the banana simply be exerting the vaginal muscles."[19]

One can only muse on the connection of this heavenly concoction of these fruits with the Ambrosia prepared for mere mortals in my Mother's kitchen. Each time she prepared it she added her own little touch. Her basic inspiration was that of Irma S. Rombauer's recipe in *The Joy of Cooking*.[20] "My roots are Victorian but I have been modernized by life and my children. My book reflects my life, and, as you may see by its timely contents, I have not stood still. So I am bringing you not only much that is old and memorable but also much that is new," Rombauer assures us in her forward. AMBROSIA. "This is an old favorite, especially popular in the South. The rule has many variations. Peel carefully, removing all membrane: 2 large Valencia oranges. Peel and cut into thin slices: 3 ripe bananas. Pineapple is sometimes added, so are other fruits. Combine and stir: 1/4 cup confectioner's sugar, 1 1/2 cups shredded coconut. Arrange alternate layers of oranges and bananas in individual serving dishes or in a bowl. Sprinkle each layer with a part of the coconut mixture, reserving some for the top. Chill the dish well before serving it."[21] Old and memorable. So it is surprising that even though the Greek poets were uncertain of the recipe, it exists in *The Joy of Cooking*. Perhaps it was found in the Ambrosian Library in Milan with that striking inscription of fico and fig eating of another kind—there with Virgil, and Homer's Odyssey in which a different kind of punishment is centered on fruit.

The story of Tantalus in torment obscures the epicurean dimensions of the crimes. Robert Graves regales us with the tale of the downfall of this would-be Master Chef. "Tantalus was the intimate friend of Zeus, who admitted him to Olympian banquets of nectar and ambrosia until, good fortune turning his head, he betrayed Zeus's secrets and stole the divine food to share among his mortal friends. Before this crime could be discovered, he committed a worse one. Having called the Olympians to a banquet, Tantalus found that the food in his larder was insufficient for the company and, either to test Zeus's omniscience, or merely to demonstrate his good will, cut up his son Pelops, and added the pieces to the stew prepared for them."[22] Condemned with a raging thirst he stands for all time in a pool that recedes when he bends to drink. His ravenous hunger for the food of the gods is his other torment. Above him a high-foliaged "tree is laden with pears, shining apples, sweet figs, ripe olives and pomegranates, which dangle against his shoulders; but whenever he reaches for the luscious fruit, a gust of wind whirls them out of reach."[23] Perhaps these are the real fruits that constitute ambrosia where the fig comes into its own and fruit combinations join mortal youths, gods and philosophers. Before considering Gide's *Fruits of the Earth* and his "Song of the Fig" and Barthes' regendering of the fruit in the thirties in all its tantalizing power, let me suggest that behind the ambrosia lies another taste for fruit. Tantalus, before Zeus, had abducted and seduced Ganymede and this must lie in part behind the pendant figs dangling against his shoulders. "Gathering fruiting branches of the wild fig" and "to squeeze figs" are allusions to the acts of the *paedicator* in Attic Greece.[24] Once Tantalus's punishment was set up, Zeus took charge of the kitchen, had Hermes collect Pelops uneaten morsels (save one shoulder that had been picked clean), and boiled them according to his own recipe. "Pelops emerged from the magic cauldron clothed in such radiant beauty (and sporting a solid ivory shoulder) that Poseidon fell in love with him on the spot, and carried him off to Olympus in a chariot drawn by golden horses. There he appointed him his cup-bearer and bed-fellow; as Zeus later appointed Ganymede, and fed him on ambrosia."[25] Fruit salad on Mount Olympus with the full fig of youth.

One would like to believe that this inspirational ambrosia tale lies behind Roland Barthes' rewriting of the *Crito* and the regenerative powers of the eating of a fig. "Sing now the fig, Simiane, because its loves are hidden,"[26] Barthes had read in Gide's *Nourritures terrestres*.[27] Barthes insists on his adolescent aversion to the fig. "There were some in the family garden in Bayonne: small, violet/purple, never ripe enough or always too ripe: sometimes the fig-milk, sometimes the rottenness disgusted me, and I never cared for this fruit. (I have since discovered them very different in Morocco and recently in the restaurant Voltaire where they are served in large soup plates of *crème fraîche*)."[28] What comes between the Roman fig—the fig-fruit of D. H. Lawrence with "sap that curdles milk and makes ricotta,/ sap that smell strange on your fingers, that even goats won't taste" embodying the female mystery and the Berber figs *(tibekhisen)* of exotic Moroccan youths is a re-gendering of the fig through a pastiche of the *Crito*. Three critical elements made this possible: his youth, Gide, and the culture of Greece. Plato, we are told, was called the *Philosukos*, the fig lover *(l'amoureux de la figue)*, but it is young Roland who has written the loveliest and most delicious text on figs and the fruits of philosophy. The story centers on how to save Socrates from death, how to take the cup of hemlock from his hands. His student, his friends want him to come away with them. Their strategy is to tempt him with figs. "Leucithes entered, carrying an array of Corinthian figs. On their sides swollen with ripeness, a few drops of glistening dew lingered; the golden skin was crackled in places revealing the rows of red seeds on a bed of white pulp. A warm sugary scent rose from the plate of clay. Socrates reached out his hand, but changing his mind 'What's the use, he said, I won't even have time to digest them.'"[29] Apollodurus spoke eloquently; then Alcibiades. He should come away with them, journey to a place where fig trees flourish. Beneath them they would sit on a terrace with benches of cool marble caressed by the salt air breezes. They would live there together, happy and wise, content with a fare of olives and figs and goat milk. Visibly moved, Socrates's heart was full. The ever practical Crito entered and knew that it was figs and not words that would turn the trick. The way was through the flesh of figs. Leucithes entered with another dish of figs. Shocked, Socrates could only stare at the array of figs before him. All eyes were on him. "They knew that the figs constituted the final assault on his virtue. If Socrates ate a fig, it would mean he had given in to their pleas. Socrates knew it too. 'We will not influence you, Socrates,' Crito said. Tiresias gently opened the window. A ray of sunshine came in caressing the figs and revealed on their golden flesh dark indentations out of which flowed a sugary warmth that intoxicated the senses. Socrates closed his eyes; it was to see the small house at Tyrinthe with its fig tree, the bench and the terrace; and he thought he could savor the taste of figs mingled with the saltier taste of the ocean air, living symbol of liberty. Then, quite simply, he reached out his hand and ate a fig."[30] Barthes asks himself what possibly could have brought him to turn the fruit of temptation, the immoral fruit, into a philosophical fruit. His answer is this: "Quite simply, undoubtedly, literature: the fig was a literary fruit, a biblical fruit, an Arcadian fruit. Unless behind the fig, there was hidden, Sex, Fica."[31]

In the end the fig is unique. One can understand its absence from the myriad recipes for fruit salads, from the fruit cocktail, from what now is passed off as Ambrosia. Despite the Muslim predilection for the banana as a tempting fruit and the light shed by candlelight coming from my own nostalgia for Mother's Candlestick Salad, and the cornucopia of fruit precariously perched on the heads of Carmen Miranda and Mickey Rooney, it is figs and fig leaves that hold my attention. I take my delight in figs. The fig, that is, that Barthes has restored to a gay Greek simplicity written across the grain of Rome and the sappiness of the fig etiquette of Lady Chatterley's closeted creator, the fig that is now a tantalizing fruit always within reach.

Notes

1. Gide, André. *Les Nourritures terrestres* in *Romans, Récits et Soties; Oeuvres lyriques* (Paris: Gallimard, Bibliotheque de la Pléiade, 1958). *Fruits of the Earth* (London: Penguin, 1970).

2. Rodgers, Bruce. *Gay Talk*. 1972 (New York: Paragon Books, 1979).

3. Random House *Historical Dictionary of American Slang*. Ed. J. E. Lighter. Vol. 1, A-G (New York: Random House, 1994).

4. Ibid., p. 84

5. Ibid., p. 85

6. Lawrence, Russell Lee. "Carmen Miranda: When Life was Just a Bowl of Cherries and Bananas and Pineapples and..." *After Dark* (May 976): 49-51.

7. Hendrickson, Robert. *Foods of Love: The Complete Guide to Aphrodisiac Edibles* (New York: Stein and Day, 1980).

8. Ibid., p. 238

9. Genesis 3:7 AV.

10. Paros, Lawrence. *The Erotic Tongue: A Sexual Lexicon* (New York: Henry Holt, 1984), p. 80.

11. Henderson, Jeffrey. *The Maculate Muse: Obscene Language in Attic Comedy* (New York and Oxford: Oxford UP, 1991), p. 116.

12. Richter, Alan. *The Language of Sexuality* (Jefferson NC and London: McFarland, 1987).

13. Lawrence, D. H. *The Complete Poems of D. H. Lawrence*, Eds. Pinto and Roberts (New York: Viking, 1969).

14. "Faire la figue à." *Nouveau Larousse Illustré*. 8 vols. (Paris: Larousse, 1897-1907).

15. Comfort, Alex. *The Joy of Sex: A Gourmet Guide to Lovemaking* (New York: A Fireside Book, Simon and Schuster, 1972).

16. Legman, Gershon. *Oral Techniques in Genital Excitement* (New York: Causeway, 1969).

17. Rombauer, Irma S. & Marion Rombauer Becker. *The Joy of Cooking*, 1931 (Indianapolis and New York: Bobbs-Merril, 1953).

18. Ibid., p. 116.

19. *Ora-genitalism*.

20. *The Joy of Cooking*.

21. Ibid., p. 749-50.

22. Graves, Robert. *The Greek Myths*. 2 vols. (Baltimore: Penguin, 1955), Vol. 2, p. 25.

23. Ibid., Vol. 2, p. 26.

24. Henderson, J. *The Maculate Muse*.

25. *The Greek Myths*, Vol. 2, p. 27.

26. Barthes, Roland. "En Marge du Criton." *L'Arc* 56 (1974): pp. 3-4.

27. *Les Nourritures terrestres*.

28. Barthes, Roland. "Premier Texte." *L'Arc* 56 (1974): pp. 4-7.

29. "En Marge," p. 4

30. Ibid., p. 7

31. "Premier Texte," p. 4.

OY

by

Clayton Eshleman

from the clear bell of O
hang a y, make it droop a bit,
tie a tail to it, can't you already hear
a tin can banging the pavement?
Joy, sadness, and enthusiasm—
                    dead image in
  living image, which is which?
Compression of oy, dead fowl in motion,
twist of oy

            "Once I saw the village butcher slice the neck of
a bird and drain the blood out of it. I wanted to cry out, but his
joyful expression caught the sound in my throat." Soutine patted
his throat and continued: "This cry, I always feel it there.
When, as a child, I drew a crude portrait of my teacher, I tried to
rid myself of this cry, but in vain. When I painted the beef
carcass it was this cry that I wanted to liberate. I have still not
succeeded."

            Oy caught in throat,
making its midnight Noah-like journey through earth & flesh,
      Soutine's *terra convulsiva* is mole
in tar, lit by a personal spectre,
  hungry, bulimic, and sincere,

or in looking at the hanging fowl,
Soutine is inside, claw twisting in a glove,
   is carcass home?
                Unending regression to get back,
to be the inside, not depict it,
hanged fowl   man hanged on his oy,
   paradise as the prism of colors
radiating through the funeral meats.

To encave the delicious pheasant,
make it a tube in which mind,
   like peristaltic jelly, can inch,

insectile whirr of broken wings,
   resurrection—
               unsure erection
hidden by the pastry chef's groin-centered
   knotted red towel.
                How empty O seems
afloat over Soutine, how it hooks down,
into the off-stage, the obscene,
into gristle bubbling with death.

I still walk my eye-stalks through these gored
   and flowering fields,
insectile pilgrim round the bend
beyond which Whitman no longer lingers—

      art as snare, or
   mantis probing, copulatory
invasion, rifted by
   galactic wind.

              [5 June 1994]

Lydia Vázquez

Ratafia and Other Love Potions

...or concerning why it is not enough
simply to know how to be a seducer—
one must also be able to carry it out!

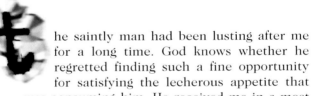

he saintly man had been lusting after me
for a long time. God knows whether he
regretted finding such a fine opportunity
for satisfying the lecherous appetite that
was consuming him. He received me in a most
Christian manner; then, after having me drink
off a glass of *ratafiat confortatif*, of which he
himself wisely drank to guard against pangs of
conscience, this accomplished libertine gener-
ously led me to his canonic bed (...). All night
long and well into the day the good priest per-
formed miracles of a nature (...). Even with all
their knowledge, neither Arétin nor Clinchtel-
Klingsted ever succeeded in inventing half the
positions and postures he had me try out; nor
were the mysteries of love ever before celebrat-
ed with more charm and in so many different
ways!

Fougeret de Monbron
Margot la Ravaudeuse[1]

Although alimentary metaphors are certainly classical, they nev-
ertheless provide the chief merit of Fougeret de Monbron's text;
this because of the way nourishment is associated with sex,

which throughout the libertine, gluttonous, and "philosophical" eighteenth century (as in the novel *Thérèse philosophe*), was more than ever the case. This "appétit devorant," developed to a lesser or greater degree, was to be a constant feature in the erotic literature of the period. Food, however, whether solid or liquid, does not merely serve to suggest the presence of something else; on the contrary, food itself is a key element in a history of sensuality that one hesitates to call 'erotic with gastronomic elements' because it sometimes proves to be gastronomy itself, lightly tinted with eroticism. As the Maréchal de Richelieu wrote, three reigns made France the nation of gastronomy, and Paris the capital of *la gourmandise:*[2] that of Louis XIV, which saw the emergence of liqueurs under the more than obliging eye of the austere Madame de Maintenon, who was herself the author of a renowned recipe for veal chops that still bears her name; that of Louis XV, following a regency under the Duc d'Orléans that was more gluttonous than epicurean; and finally that of Louis XVI, full of cafés and restaurants. By the mid-eighteenth century culinary habits had been almost completely transformed by the now habitual consumption of foods from overseas. While alchemy operated on the level of bodies, which—according to the theory of humors—could be either hot or cold, dry or humid, or a combination, it also goes hand in hand with an alchemy of kitchens and wine cellars, and this for everyone's benefit. Thus ratafia,[3] which Dejean called a "panacea," in his 1769 *Traité raisonée de la distillation*, attributing "prodigious and marvelous effects" to it, made its entry into the eighteenth century's *soupers fins*; and if one is to take him at his word, it was thanks to ratafia that the Canon St. Nicholas became Margot's new master. Of similar efficacy are chocolate, coffee, tobacco, tea, various spices, champagne, the wines of Burgundy (to the detriment of Bordeaux), Spanish wines such as Rota, Malaga, Sherry and the strange case of Alicante; Tokay wine, Lacrima-Christi, all liqueurs, fish (some of which, such as crayfish and raw oysters, had only recently been discovered to have aphrodisiac powers),[4] poultry, certain fruits and vegetables, and finally cookies and sweets (such as blanc-mange) and deserts in general. What all these aliments have in common is their action as "confortatifs" or, to use a more "medical" expression, such as the one used by Lémery, they "arouse the seed."[5]

With their "warming" effects, these aliments would soon become familiar to the libertine marquis of French novels. As aspiring seducers not always physically equal to the circumstances, they will make frequent use of them, whether it be before making love to their "victims," or to excite themselves or their victim, as did Canon St. Nicholas with Margot (although more often it occurs within the context of a *souper galant*), or whether it be to regain the strength lost after bouts of valiant love-making, which, alas, are often just the prelude to an excessively long evening.

However, it must be stated that this libertine-seducer, although making his first novelistic appearance during the regency period in the works of Crebillon *fils*, will have no need of such rejuvenating "tonics" until quite a bit later. As Henri Lafon has emphasized,[6] it is not until the second half, even the last part of the century that the heroes of French novels are seen eating, and, as I will demonstrate, in our case eating in order to strengthen themselves. Is the Frenchman of the end of the century as masculine as his ancestor of the preceding one? I have no doubt that he is. Rather, what we have here is a curious case of crossbreeding, within a single species of literature, of two fundamentally distinct philosophies; one libertine and epicurean, proper to the courtesans of the first half of the century, and the other Laclosian or Rousseauist, defending the world of nature and a healthy and strong body, although adapted to the libertine aesthetic of the end of the century.

Grimod de la Reynière and Jean-Anthelme Brillat-Savarin,[7] the two chroniclers of eighteenth century gastronomy, offer a poetic and anecdotal panorama of the foods—from fruits and vegetables, fish and meat, to wines and other "spirits," as the Englishmen in French novels of the period call them—for the invigoration of our taste, smell, and sight... as well as our "generative drive." It is no accident that Brillat-Savarin, in his first "Meditation," entitled "The Senses," adds a sixth sense to the five traditional ones: to sight, smell, hearing, touch and taste he adds "generative drive" or "physical love," "which draws the sexes toward one another, and the aim of which is the reproduction of the species."[8] Only Buffon, in passing, took note of this sense, himself associating it with taste, sight, and smell. For while the "aphrodisiac" effects of the above-mentioned foods are immediately apparent (otherwise they would not have been mentioned!), the causes are variable: their "juices" (some warming, affecting warm and cold bodies; others drying, affecting moist and humidified bodies; still others moistening, affecting dry bodies, i.e. "mummies") stimulate the sense of taste and cause "fire to course through the veins."[9] At the center of an empassioned sensory practice lies the power of heat and cold, undoubtedly because of the popularity of the theory of the humors: coffee, hot chocolate, and tea become fashionable not only because they are stimulants that come from exotic plants imported from the colonies, but also because they are drunk very hot; on the other hand, ice cream too becomes the rage, kept cold at the table with snow, such as the one the Caliph in *Vathek* tastes, causing him to forget about everything but love.[10] The colors of a fruit, especially red, such as the red of a strawberry, are especially coveted, although this particular passion provokes an ironic smile from the lips of certain cosmopolitans who see themselves as above this type of rather bourgeois "novelty." It was the Prince de Ligne, an enthusiast of word play, who, in reply to a question about his taste for strawberries, answered that he preferred "frambaises,[11] whose forms are more seductive to the gaze, as were those of the omelet that made Madame Récamier famous.[12] Their perfumes are a veritable balm, to the point sometimes, as in the case of saffron, of offending the sense of smell (indeed, if not for its ability to ward off the blindness that sometimes comes with syphilis, saffron would not be recommended).

Cultural and sociological reasons also play an important role: a Western tradition born of an alimentary temptation and a certain aphrodisiac culture is perhaps at the root of Caraccioli's assertion that "apples ward off melancholy,"[13] or of the importance of hydromel or hypocras, which the Greeks and Romans apparently knew about. The exoticism of certain foods (*Vathek's* rice with almond juice and cinnamon), the rarity of others, their refinement or great cost are sometimes the simple source of the nervousness felt about ingesting them; for example, a virgin cock, the thigh of a quail, on which it stands when sleeping (Brillat-Savarin), or the "purée of humming-bird egg" that the King of Erzb-can paid a hundred thousand ecus for in order to please the kind Arsénide.[14] Other foods are preferred because they can be easily transported and consumed which, it must be admitted, is a great advantage when lovers find themselves in situations that are not very convenient for eating: this is what happened with the Knight of Aiglemont, locked in *Felicia's* wardrobe,[15] to whom "poultry, wine and fruit" were brought as "restoratives," being foods that can be hidden without much difficulty and eaten cold. The lightness of foods, during a period in which stoutness was no longer fashionable and anglophilia had changed people's culinary habits, put steamed foods on the agenda and, most importantly, made dinner a more important meal than supper. This fashion for light foods also limited the choice of restoratives, and poultry occupied an extremely important place, even in the menus of the Marquis de Sade's *120 Days of Sodom*.[16] Poultry is light because it flies and this lightness is felt by those who eat it. Given this imaginative outlook, what could be less surprising than to find our seducers consuming, by analogy, stag meat, an animal reputed to be "unbridled"? Finally, certain libertines, enthusiasts of any and all types of subversive decadence, of reason subverted by the strange, were drawn to sorcery and other forms of "deviltry": the firmness of Révéroni Saint-Cyr's affirmation, concerning an act of symbolic communion with one of Biondetta's successors, touches the heart of the matter: "Like rabies, love is a feverish rage, and its infection is spread just like the disease, by the bite. Diet: charred turtledove bone, camphor and snake skin. Treatment: constant biting."[17]

Does imagination play an important role in the composition of these love potions? Of course it does, but this in no way invalidates the value of dishes accompanied by rich beverages which, for the first time in the "classical" novel, now appear in large numbers. As Henri Lafon points out, as late as 1735, Bougeant, in his *Amazing Voyage of Prince Fan-Fédérin in Romancie*,[18] is still surprised to see "how princes and princesses, heroes and their heroines, domestics and even entire royal retinues live their whole lives without ever talking about eating and drinking."

Nevertheless, the repertory of these "stimulants of the passions of Venus" (to use Lémery's words) remains rather limited; with rare exceptions, the authors of our novels use the same culinary ingredients. Quantities aside (let us not forget the fourteen courses of the famous suppers served by Grimod de la Reynière, beginning on the First of February, 1783), the fact that the "libertine cuisine" of the eighteenth century is easily reproducible can only add to its attractiveness for the twentieth century reader.

Following Grimod, Brillat-Savarin, and the anonymous author of *La cuisine et l'amour*, together with our novels, we can draw up a list of ingredients; of the aphrodisiacs of the vegetable kingdom: mint, pepper, mustard (Maille's recipe, for Grimod), watercress, celery, artichokes and asparagus, nutmeg, pimento, thyme, clove, vanilla, cocoa, saffron, truffles, orange, as well as certain flowers, such as the violet, which, when its leaves are candied, can be eaten as a delicacy. From the animal kingdom: poultry (particularly white meat) is preferred—in general feathered game is favored over the hair-growing kind, which is more difficult to digest; mutton and veal is chosen rather than beef and pork, fish (from rivers, smoked or salted), and crustaceans, of which lobster, crayfish, mollusks, oysters and other bivalves are preferred. Fresh eggs are eaten too, but cooked rather than swallowed raw. Among drinks: eau-de-vie, hot chocolate, coffee and tea, wines (especially Champagne and foreign vintages with high alcohol content), cider and beer, although these last two are in lesser repute. Tobacco is once more a solid part of social custom, although it is thought to be more "stimulating" when smoked than snorted or chewed. Amber, chives, musks, the various cantharides, opiates and substances compounded of these elements and taken in pill form are considered "positive aphrodisiacs" and therefore dangerous: although often encountered in the pornographic literature of the period, they are not recommended by any knowledgeable authorities on alimentation. Let us now summarize the most frequently consumed stimulants and restoratives found in the novels of the period: among the collations that can be drunk "at all times" coffee is number one: we are still in the period of coffee's flowering, of the deepening of the knowledge of "mocha." Brillat-Savarin reports on how coffee was first discovered: "An ancient tradition states that coffee was discovered by a shepherd who realized that his herd became especially excited and gay whenever it grazed on the berries of coffee plants."[19] He adds that coffee produces insomnia but that "the insomnia caused by coffee is not painful; one's perceptions are very clear and there's no desire to sleep: that's all!"[20] What a godsend for our seducers! There is thus nothing surprising in finding La Morlière's hero, under an evil spell, praying to the genie Mocha to help him stay awake when he's with his mistress so that he can finally fulfill his duty.[21]

All in all, however, it is chocolate, both in society and in literature, that becomes the food "emblematic of the new, janus-faced society, both nervous and lazy, lively and lifeless, diligent and voluptuous, surrendering to tardy awakenings and predawn bustlings."[22] There is not enough space here to enumerate all the heroes, the out of breath seducers for whom chocolate was a lifesaver. One need only leaf through *The Manuscript Found at Saragossa* to see that chocolate is the fundamental source of "health and vigor,"[23] both restorative and stimulative, and democratic in the sense that we see it, either taken or offered, by bohemians, laborers and nobles. At the same time it can be the most refined of delicacies, especially in the form of "chocolate *esponjado*," a mixture of Alicante wine, chocolate, bread and eggs.

Since we have come to the subject of alcoholic drinks and to Alicante itself, I will not deny that for the longest time I was unable to disguise my astonishment at the almost incomprehensible importance accorded to this wine in the novels of the period. On the same level as the great Burgundies and the best Champagnes, and superior to other foreign wines for its aphrodisiac powers (comparable to the those of the best eaux-de vie), the reason for this preference would seem to be of a cultural nature. Apparently, because it was heavily perfumed and of relatively low quality Alicante wine was used by the Romans as a fragrant liquid; it was mixed with vanilla and nutmeg cloves for the bath taken by a man on the night before his wedding. This is probably the source of its reputation as a stimulant, and its ingestion was probably a result of rumors that arose in relation to this usage. However, we now know that there exists a wine, called *fondillon*, that is produced exclusively around the city of Alicante: harvested in extremely small quantities, high in alcohol content and with undeniable restorative qualities, it was already appreciated at the time by the Grandees of the Spanish court and their European friends. During the *souper galant*, which took place relatively late, the Bresse pullet took center stage, even when compared with oysters, of which several gross had to be eaten in order to satisfy one's appetite at a single sitting (it appears that it was impossible to reach satiety regardless of the number of oysters consumed). This is precisely what happens to a couple described by Brillat-Savarin, who, having dined on several gross of oysters and later a supper of soup, arose at two in the morning, to have a bite to eat because they were hungry. After consuming a "lovely" and "snow-white" Bresse pullet the Lady returned to bed only to awake in the morning to two coughing fits and a bout of blushing.[24] All the experts agreed that the wing of the chicken was the most delicate part, and the white the most restorative. Once again we have the same question as for Alicante wine, and the same dead end. Thus I find myself obliged to offer a whimsical and charming explanation for this belief, in part provided by the anonymous author of *Un Voyageur à Paris*,[25] who informs us that "chicken" is a synonym for "love letter," a designation derived from Italian hen houses, where seducers would buy fat chickens to send as a gift to their mistresses, a love letter under the wing, pasted to the white meat!

The eighteenth century saw a new wave of interest in fish, due in part to greater culinary exchange with other European countries that consumed more fish than France, particularly Spain and Italy; other causes included the fashion for light foods and the reputation of fish for increasing sexual powers, with which all food experts agreed. Within the world of fish, the raw product (as a source of phosphorous) wins out over the cooked, which in part explains the preference for oysters and crayfish; eel being the one exception because it was the probable cause of death—by indigestion—of Frederick II, who had the misfortune of temporarily neglecting French cuisine in favor of a German recipe.

Truffles deserve a chapter unto themselves. So popular were they that it is difficult to find a single recipe of the period, whether for fish or meat, that does not include them. As a basic ingredient in any elaborate food cooked up in the novels of the period, the truffle—whether black or white, although the Perigord variety would appear to be the preferred type—tends to cause those who eat it to lose all will, engaging in acts for which they will have cause to regret on the following day:

> The centerpiece of our supper, which in all other respects was light, was a superb truffled fowl(...). The truffles were especially delicious, and you know how I love them: nevertheless, I controlled myself; moreover, I limited myself to a single glass of champagne (...) Verseuil was alternately flattering, expansive, affectionate, tender (...). He persisted in acting in a way that had the potential of becoming completely offensive; I was hard put to bring him to his senses(...). Finally, he left; I went to bed (...). But the next morning was the Day of Judgment: examining my behavior of the night before, I found it reprehensible. I should have stopped Verseuil at his first protestations, I should not have taken part in a conversation that boded only ill. My pride should have been wakened earlier, my eyes should have frowned severely on him; I should have rung for help, shouted, gotten angry: I should have done everything I did not do. What can I say to you, Sir? I blame it all on the truffles.[26]

However, not everything is a love potion; neither all wines nor all chocolates. Indeed, says Mercier,[27] adulterated wines unfortunately abound, as in Félicia. Often this adulteration amounts to poisoning, which was the obsessive fear of Frenchmen mixing with Spanish and Italian women, who because of their passionate nature, were thought of as correspondingly fatal cooks; and indeed, poison was served in a bowl reserved for chocolate.[28] Moreover, excess consumption of wine, liqueurs and even chocolate was believed to produce an anaphrodisiac effect: the fear of this condition restored the good sense and sobriety to several literary personages, including Casanova's Edouard (in *l'Icosaméron*), the French adventurers of Lesuire, and Voisenon's Sultan Misapouf, all of whom became vegetarians.

Milk drinkers, the very apotheosis of the sober-minded, find themselves depicted positively by Casanova in the persons of the Mecramigues (this in spite of the fact that, in general, a taste for milk expresses sexual impotence, as in the case of the poor husband of Vivant Denon's *Point de Lendemain*).[29] These heroes, embodiments of a frugal virtue, are perhaps also a specular reflection of someone like Rétif de la Bretonne (see *Monsieur Nicolas*), who was an enthusiast of lentils, which were reputed to have anaphrodisiac qualities; or of Cagliostro's cheese eaters, who represent for the French imagination the kind of very virile European whose appetites—already well awakened by Nature—need to be calmed rather than excited.

However, the prodigious apart, today, as in the past, men are always needing ways to improve their sexual performance, since their reputation as seducers—and this is no small matter!—is at stake. Are these various treatments, such as ratafia and other love potions really effective? What does it matter! They were effective enough to put imagination and "good taste" into eighteenth century French cuisine, effective enough to make possible the amazing feats performed by the seducers of—alas—another era. But let us not be too skeptical. It is true that Tissot warns us that men of letters are subject to an additional loss of seminal force, which exacerbates our case. In any event, Grimod advises if these remedies have no effect, to take cold baths, "which harden the solid parts." And if absolutely nothing works, as the author of *La Cuisine et l'amour* writes, if we cannot be with the desired person twice a day, we will at least be together once a day, to eat and to eat well.

Translated by Thomas Epstein

Notes

1. Fougeret de Monbron. *Margot la Ravaudeuse*. The circulation of the anonymous manuscript led to its author's arrest in 1748. Ed. Paris, Zulma, 1992, with a preface and commentary by Michel Delon. pp. 50-51.
2. *Vie privée du maréchal de Richelieu*, Paris, Desjonquères, 1993, trad. de la rééd. italienne de B. Craveri, Adelphi, ed., 1989, p. 23.
3. From the Latin *rata fiat*, "Let the transaction be completed," attested in 1675; it was drunk at the notary's office to celebrate the conclusion of an accord between two parties; a mixture of eau-de-vie, sugar and wine, Champagne or Burgundy (in the eighteenth century, it more generally meant eau-de-vie, sugar and fruits.
4. Vid. Anonyme. *La cuisine et l'amour*, s.d. Bibl. Nationale de Paris 8 V, pp. 32-34.

5. Louis Lémery. *Traité des Alimens*, Paris 2e éd., chez P. Witte, 1705.

6. Henri Lafon. "Du thème alimentaire dans le roman," *Dix-Huitième*, no. 14, 1975.

7. Grimod de la Reynière. *Almanachs and other Écrits gastronomiques* rééd. Paris, UGE, 10/18, 1977. In 1825 Jean-Anthelme Brillat-Savarin wrote his *Physiologie du gout* (rééd. Paris, Champs/Flammarion, 1982), summarizing the history of French culinary art of the preceding century.

8. Brillat-Savarin, op. cit., p. 39.

9. Jan Potocki. *Manuscrit trouvé à Saragosse*, rééd. Paris, J. Corti, 1989. p.115. 10. Beckford, W. Vathek, conte arabe, rééd. Paris, J. Corti, 1984, p. 134.

11. Word play on *"fraise"* (strawberry), *"framboise"* (rasberry) and *"baiser,"* to kiss or (vulg.) fuck. Prince de Ligne: Memoires, lettres et pensées, rééd. préfacée par Chantal Thomas, Paris, F. Bourin, 1989. "Mémoires," p. 288.

12. This anecdote is reported by Brillat-Savarin, who gives the recipe for a tuna omelet made by a priest for Mme Récamier, who praised it all over Paris for its "shape, its roundness, and its size." Brillat-Savarin, op. cit., p. 309: "L'Omelette du curé."

13. Louis Antoine de Caraccioli. *De la Gaieté*, Paris, Chez Nyon, 1762, p. 289

14 La Morlière. *Angola, Histoire indienne*, rééd. in *Romans libertins du XVIIIe siècle*, Bouquins, Paris, Laffont, p. 384.

15. Andréa de Nerciat. *Félicia ou mes fredaines* in *Romans libertins du XVIIIe siècle*, op. cit., p. 1098.

16. D.A.F. de Sade. *Les cent-vingt journées de Sodome*, in *Oeuvres*, La Pléiade, vol. I, éd. critique par Michel Delon, Paris, Gallimard, 1990.

17. Révéroni Saint-Cyr. *Pauliska ou la perversité moderne*, rééd. Paris, Desjonquères, 1991; éd. établie par Michel Delon, p. 58.

18. Henri Lafon. "Du thème alimentaire dans le roman," *Dix-Huitième*, no. 14, 1975.

19. Brillat-Savarin. *Physiologie du goût*, pp. 111-112

20. Ibid, p. 114.

21. La Morlière. *Angola*, in *Romans libertins du XVIIIe siècle*, pp. 477-478.

22. Piero Camporesi. *Le Gout du chocolat*, trad. Paris, Grasset 1992.

23. J. Potocki. *Manuscrit trouvé à Saragosse*.

24. Brillat-Savarin. *Physiologie du goût*.

25. Anonyme. *Un Voyageur à Paris*, Paris 3 Tomes/1 vol., 1797, p. 62

26. Brillat-Savarin. *Physiologie du goût*.

27. Louis Sebastien Mercier. *Tableau de Paris*, Vol. 2.

28. A. de Nerciat. *Félicia ou mes fredaines* in *Romans libertins du XVIII siècle*; J. Potocki. *Manuscrit trouvé à Saragosse*.

29. Vivant Denon. *Point du Lendemain* in *Romanciers du XVIIIe siècle*, Paris, La Pléiade, vol. 2.

Jeanne Dunning, *Sample 9,* 1996. Cibachrome mounted to plexiglass, frame, ed. of 3, 21-3/4 x 19-1/2 in. Courtesy Feigen Contemporary, NYC.

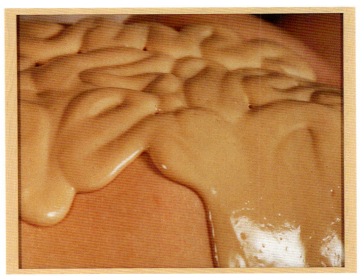

Jeanne Dunning, *The Edible 1*, 1997. Cibachrome mounted to plexiglass and frame, ed. 1/5, 26 x 32 in. Courtesy Feigen Contemporary, NYC.

Jeanne Dunning, *The White*, 1996. Cibachrome mounted to plexiglass, frame, edition 2/3. 73-1/2 x 51-1/12 in. Courtesy Feigen Contemporary, NYC.

Rob Wynne, "Let Simmer for 3 or 4 Mins...", 1996. Black and white photograph with text embroidered on felt, 30 x 28 in. Courtesy Holly Solomon Gallery, NYC.

Rob Wynne, *Picnic*, 1992. Photo on linen and fabric, 90 x 60 in. Courtesy Holly Solomon Gallery, NYC.

Chrysanne Stathacos & Hunter Reynolds, *The Banquet*, 1992. Installation. Robert J. Shiffler Collection & Archive, Greenville, Ohio. Photo Maxine Henryson.

Chrysanne Stathacos & Hunter Reynolds, *The Banquet*, 1-5-92. Nude Man Reclining on Banquet Table surrounded by food during performance. Courtesy Robert J. Shiffler Collection and Archive. Photo Robbie Lourenzo.

Chrysanne Stathacos & Hunter Reynolds, *The Banquet*, 1-5-92. Nude Man Reclining on Banquet Table surrounded by food during performance. Courtesy the Robert J. Shiffler Collection and Archive. Photo Robbie Lourenzo.

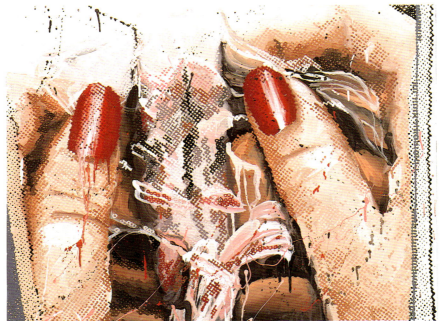

Marilyn Minter, *100 Food Porn #61*, 1990. Enamel on metal sign, 24 x 30 in. Courtesy Xavier Laboulbenne Gallery. Photo Dennis Cowley.

Marilyn Minter, *100 Food Porn #90*, 1990. Enamel on metal sign, 24 x 30 in. Courtesy Xavier Laboulbenne Gallery.

Marilyn Minter, *100 Food Porn #45*, 1990. Enamel on metal sign, 24 x 30 in. Courtesy Xavier Laboulbenne Gallery.

Marilyn Minter, *100 Food Porn #95*, 1990. Enamel on metal sign, 24 x 30 in. Courtesy Xavier Laboulbenne Gallery.

GASTRO-ETHNICITY

In fact, considerably more of the faithful than we imagine instinctively frequent those parishes where the Host are of the best repute. This mania on the part of the Lovers of the Host is of a clandestine nature. The greater public can only guess at the excesses. All that is known is that those people hide their ugly passion, and that they form a secret clan at the very heart of the Church.

These connoisseurs appear to be demanding. They are, in fact. They judge, without any possible appeal, the quality of the dough and the baking, the purity of the contour, in short, the quality of everything that incites the admiration of the Host of the *first quality* .

They have a rule never to compromise on its roundness, wishing it to have the perfection of a circle. They are horrified by lumps, and they condemn all dough that is insufficiently smooth. The Communicant who represents the Order has but to notice a malformation so that, upon his signal they all leave the place. This Order of the Lovers of the Host is powerful. It has its hierarchies and its initation rites. It is an occult force within the State. The tragedy is that its affiliates are a core within the Elite. A single condemnation recently sufficed to destroy the reputation of a solidly established parish. Its habitués immediately deserted it for the sake of another, "where after all," as they say, "quality still triumphs."

To test, to compare the different sorts of Hosts from one parish to another is a matter of an hour or two of careful tasting. This task is relegated to emissaries whose taste and experience are acknowledged by all. Once the best parish is announced, normally by leaflet, the flock runs there in a stampede.

The vicar congratulates himself on this revival of the Faith which he relies on for his promotion. He is fooling himself. For it is in fact quite rare that the Lovers of the Host settle down.

Michel Maxence
"The Lovers of the Host"

Allen S. Weiss

The Ideology of the Pot-au-feu

he very name *pot-au-feu*—pot-in-the-fire, fire-pot, the empty vessel in the flame—indicates the primal condition of cuisine, its empty form, its symbolic zero-degree of signification. Thus the sundry poetic and political peregrinations of this dish of boiled beef and vegetables in their consommé should come as no surprise.

This tale begins several years ago, in the Lyonnais restaurant Léon de Lyon, where I dined with two friends, both eighteenth century specialists, and one furthermore a scholar of nineteenth century gastronomy. It happens that two of us chose the same dish, but for different reasons: cabbage stuffed with fois gras, truffles, sweetbreads and cockscombs. I absolutely had to try this haute cuisine invention for sheerly nostalgic reasons, as stuffed cabbage is the national dish of my father's birthplace, Hungary; my friend wanted to try it for reasons of intellectual curiosity, since the ingredients were those of the *petits soupers* of the Ancien Régime. As for my second companion, she looked at us in amazement for having ordered such a bizarre concoction, and proceeded to ask for a simple pot-au-feu, in my eyes the most banal, traditional dish on the menu. Afterwards, she insisted that it was "transubstantial." Our mutual incomprehension might well allegorize a seismic symbolic rift in the history of modern French culture.

In his classic *Physiologie du goût* (1825), Jean-Anthelme Brillat-Savarin writes of the mysterious *osmazôme*, a sort of essence composed of the reduced juices of red meat. The symbolic implications of osmazôme are characterized by Roland Barthes in his preface to Brillat-Savarin's book: "Faithful to his philosophy of essences, Brillat-Savarin attributes a sort of spiritual power to osmazôme. As the word is masculine, it is the very absolute of taste, a sort of meat alcohol. As a universal (demoniacal?) principle, it takes on varied and seductive appearances: it is what makes the roux of meats, the crustiness of roasts, the scent of game. And it is especially that which makes gravy and bouillon, those direct forms of quintessence (the etymology of the word goes back to the related idea of odor and bouillon.)"[1] The description of this essence serves as the introduction to the very first dish listed among the specialties discussed by Brillat-Savarin, the pot-au-feu. And yet, while he emphasizes its dietary values, he immediately reveals his estimation of this dish by describing, with the sarcasm that greatly contributed toward the fame of his book, the sorts of people who enjoy eating boiled beef: people of habit, who eat it because their parents ate it, and whose children will therefore eat it; impatient people, who are always ready to jump on the first dish set before their eyes; inattentive people, who regard dining as an obligatory duty, and thus put themselves at the same level as what they eat; and finally, people of huge appetite, who simply devour their food.[2] Indeed, the critique of the pot-au-feu is based on a negative corollary derived from the notion of the consommé as essence, i.e., the fact that boiled beef is the flesh minus its juice. The core of the pot-au-feu thus exists minus its essential component. As Brillat-Savarin notes, such dishes have disappeared from fine meals.

Brillat-Savarin's critique thus sets the stage for the elimination of the pot-au-feu from the annals of haute cuisine. For Escoffier—the chef who codified and collated the great recipes of the nineteenth century, those which would become the basis of French haute cuisine for nearly three quarters of a century— would, in a curious nominal slippage, suppress this dish in his classic book, *Le guide culinaire* (1903). He opens his discourse at the same point as Brillat-Savarin: at the very beginning of his book, where he discusses the "Fundamental Elements of Cooking," he lists "The Principal Kinds of Fonds de Cuisine" (foundation sauces and stocks), which begins with ordinary and clarified consommés. One might thus expect that this place of honor would valorize the prime representative of the consommé, the pot-au-feu, but the fact is otherwise. For turning to recipe #599 *Pot-au-Feu*, one reads: "Prepare exactly like the *petite marmite.*" The actual instructions are given in recipe #598 *La Petite Marmite.* In this bible of haute cuisine, the pot-au-feu is deprived of its recipe and reduced to a pure name. This suppression is symptomatic of the direction of French gastronomy at the turn of the century, exemplified by the ascendance of Escoffier's cooking in the chain of hotels created by César Ritz, the summit of international luxury and decadence. The simple pot-au-feu, the family dish par excellence, would have little place in the complex, changing, inventive, often abstract and occasionally absurd cuisine of the upper classes. And yet, precisely because of its traditional symbolic value and its very inappropriateness in the context of haute cuisine, the pot-au-feu would play an equally important symbolic role in the development of a reactionary literature, which celebrates a return to the French earth and the Catholic Church as the only means of salvation from a modernism whose revaluation of all values was seen by many as the ultimate catastrophe.

The text on the back cover of a recent edition of Joris-Karl Huysman's *Là-bas* (1891)—the tale of a man whose research on Gilles de Rais brings him into contact with both satanic ritual and Catholic belief—offers the following synopsis: "Black masses and satanic invocations follow, organized by an excommunicated priest, the Canon Docre, who had the image of the cross drawn on the soles of his feet so as to constantly trample it, and whose most innocent pleasure is to feed the consecrated host to white mice. In this world of sabbaths and blasphemy, reason takes refuge in a tower of the church of Saint-Sulpice, where, for the sake of a few rare survivors, the wife of the bellringer cooks up a divine pot-au-feu."[3] The principle theological issue at stake—the eternal battle between good and evil, as it is manifested in the contemporary French Catholic milieu—is here symbolized in culinary terms: the struggle between the life giving principles of moral purity open to man (symbolized by the pot-au-feu), and the satanic traps of the Devil (who desecrates the host) in the form of one of his avatars, the mouse. The presentation of the pot-au-feu in the dining room of the belltower, serves as one of the key moments of the narrative; here, one finds both a critique of modern urban culture and a celebration of the values (family values!) essential to the reactionary religious sentiments of the day. "This lodging was quite poor, but so very cordial, cozy, pleasant! Especially the rural table setting, the clean glasses, the dish of fresh salted butter, the jug of cider, all of which added to the intimacy of the table, lit by a slightly worn lamp that spread its tarnished silver gleam on the coarse tablecloth."[4] The simple, healthful, pure pleasures of the countryside are transported into a sacred urban space, a site of repose and communion within an otherwise fallen city. In this microcosm, even the presence of lamplight, in an epoch of rampant electrification, adds to the symbolic scenario. And then there is the meal, consisting of a pot-au-feu, a simple salad, and cider. "'This time it's a success!' exclaimed his wife, while serving each person a bouillon the color of mahogany, its surface a moiré of bronze waves, bubbling with topaz eyes. It was succulent and unctuous, robust and yet delicate, refined as it was by the addition of boiled chicken innards. Everybody was now silent, their noses in their plates, their faces kindled by fumigations from the aromatic soup."[5]

Immediately, this welcoming dish became the pretext for a vicious critique of restaurants and all that they imply, by Durtel, one of the guests, who describes a restaurant in Paris where he goes about once a month, certain that this establishment is guilty of poisoning its clients: "While nibbling at the sauce gratinée of a redoubtable sole, I observed the customers who surrounded me, and I found them singularly changed since my last visit. They had either lost weight or were bloated; their eyes were either hollow and ringed with violet or sagging under double rose pouches; the fat people had turned yellow; the skinny ones green... This interested me, as you can well imagine, and I made myself into a course in toxicology and discovered, by studying myself while eating, the frightful ingredients that masked the taste of disinfected fish as well as of cadavers, powdery mixtures of carbon and tan, meats disguised by marinades, painted with sauces the color of sewers, wines colored with fuchsine, perfumed with furfural, and thickened with molasses and plaster."[6] Soon afterwards, the evocation of blasphemy permits what had begun as a moralizing contrast between the natural and the artificial, the rural and the urban, to devolve into a discussion of the ultimate opposition between the sacred and the diabolic. In the context of his research on Gilles de Rais, the protagonist, des Hermies, offers a brief genealogy of satanism in France, specifically mentioning certain black masses of the seventeenth century celebrated by the Abbot Guibourg on the nude bodies of women, masses in which such notables of the royal court as Madame de Montespan were said to have participated. "The ritual of these ceremonies was quite atrocious; generally, a child was carried off, and then burned in an oven in the countryside; then the remaining powder was mixed with the blood of another child whose throat had been slashed, so as to obtain a paste resembling that used by the Manicheans I told you about. The Abbot Guibourg officiated, consecrating the host by cutting it up into little pieces and mixing it with this blood darkened by ash; such was the matter of the Holy Sacrament."[7] To add to this horror—where desecration is predicated upon the death of innocents; and where the sacred host, which should never even touch the teeth for fear of injury, is sliced up with a knife—is yet another form of Black Mass, the Mass of Sperm. The transubstantiation of the host is abjected by its satanic simulacra; the spiritual life-giving host is replaced by the visceral marks of a sinful eroticism and an unholy death.

In this context, the symbolic articulation of Là-bas puts tremendous allegorical importance on the pot-au-feu, as the culinary point of sanity and purity in an increasingly decadent world. Indeed, the last chapter of the book begins with another meal in the belltower, where Madame Carhaix offers her guests the bouillon of the pot-au-feu that was made the night before. This bouillon, served with noodles, is at the center of the meal, accompanied by a salad of cold meat mixed with sour herring and celery, a purée of potatoes and cheese, and dessert, all washed down with new cider. Durtal and des Hermies exclaim that her cooking is an incitement to the sin of gluttony, yet this joke is but an ironic prefiguration of yet another gastronomic metaphor, with which the novel concludes, expressing the full force of Huysmans's pessimism and anti-modernism: "...this century doesn't give a damn about Christ in Glory; it contaminates the supernatural and vomits it out. How then can we have hope for the future, how can we imagine that the children born of those fetid bourgeois in these filthy times will be clean? Brought up in that way, I wonder what they will accomplish in life." Durtal replies: "They will do like their fathers, like their mothers. They will stuff their bellies and they will empty out their souls through their guts!"[8] This excremental vision, couched in the vilest of alimentary terms, is all the more forceful for the divine pot-au-feu which they are already digesting as they speak.

The symbolic destiny of the pot-au-feu takes a lighter, though not much less conservative, turn in Marcel Rouff's beloved novel, *La vie et la passion de Dodin-Bouffant, Gourmet* (1924), a book dedicated to several great gastronomes, both living and dead: Brillat-Savarin, Curnonsky, Gabion, Guy de Pourtalès. In this tale of two meals, the protagonist, the great gourmet Dodin-Bouffant, is invited to a dinner hosted by the Prince of Eurasia, who wishes to absolutely astonish his guests with the most perfect and extravagant meal ever conceived. In a pastiche of the nineteenth century French haute cuisine brought to its apogée by Carême, this feast, served in the already outmoded manner of the *service à la française* (several courses, each composed of many dishes presented simultaneously), is a veritable compendium of the sort of cooking codified by Escoffier.

First Course:
Soups:
Bisque de pigeon
Bisque de cailles au coulis à la reine
Bisque d'écrevisses
Bisque de soles farcies

Center Dish:
Marcassin

End Dishes:
Pâté royal
Terrine de faisans aux truffes vertes

Hors-d'oeuvres:
Perdreaux aux fines herbes à la broche, avec une essence de
jambon
Poupetin de tourterelles
Saucissons à la dauphine
Brochet fourré

Large Main Dishes:
Poulardes farcies à la crème
Lapereaux à la Saingaraz
Oiseaux de rivière accommodés aux huitres

Wines for the first course: Dry Sherry after the soups; whites:
Carbonnieux, Langon, Meursault, Pouilly; reds: La Chaînette,
Thorins, Saint-Estèphe; between the first and second courses,
Malvasia from Cyprus and Madeira.

Second Course:
Fish:
Lottes du lac de Genève à la vestale
Truites de torrent à la Chartreuse

Large Roasts:
Dindons à la daube
Côtes de boeuf à la hollandaise
Poitrine de veau au pontif, escortée de ris de veau et de
quenelles
Gigot de mouton en filets farcis

Sauces:
Piquante
Au pauvre homme
Au bleu celeste
À la nichon

Salads:
D'herbes
D'oranges
D'olives

Side Dishes:
Chanterelles farcies
Crêtes en pagode au vin de Champagne
Asperges
Rôties en rocher
Laitances de carpes à la Béchamel
Truffes à la Maréchale

Wines: whites: Haut-Preignac, Muscat de Frontignan, Jurançon, Seyssel; reds: Côte-Saint-Jacques, Cortaillod-en-Neuchâtel, Richebourg, Romanée-Conti; between the second and third courses: Tokay, grenache, lacryma-christi, and sorbets au marasquin.

Third Course:
Soups:
Panade de blancs de poulardes
Bouillon de métonnage
Ouille au bain-marie

Main Dishes:
Hure de saumon
Lapins au Père Douillet
Oie à la carmagnole
Alouettes au gratin
Faisan en gondole
Terrine de bécasses

Hors-d'oeuvres:
Andouilles de poisson
Beignets de blanc-manger
Foie gras à la cendre

Desserts:
Compote de coings en gelée vermeille
Compote grillée de pêches
Pâtes d'avelines
Marmelade de violettes
Oranges douces et des poires à l'eau-de-vie
Candis de cannelle et de jonquille
Gaufres au vin d'Espagne

Allen S. Weiss

Cornets et des gimblettes
Massepains en laqs d'amour
Macarons au liquide
Glaces de rose, d'épine-vinette et de grenade
Ouvrages d'amande
Fromages glacés
Eaux de fenouil, de pistache, et d'orgeat

Wines: whites: Yvorne, Rochecorbon, Puy-Notre-Dame, Vouvray; reds: Chambertin, Mouton-Lafite, Hermitage, Lunel; red Champagnes of Bouzy and Verzeney, and Port; followed by coffee, ratafias blancs d'abricots de Grenoble, muscat, anis.

Then it is Dodin-Bouffant's turn. Needless to say, his estimation of the Prince's meal is best summed up by the menu he had his cook, Adèle Pidou, create in reciprocation for the Prince's gargantuan and ridiculous effort. This meal—presented in the modern *service à la russe,* where one dish follows another—speaks for itself, especially given its centerpiece, which at this point can be easily intuited by the reader:

Friandises avant le potage
Potage Adèle Pidou
Fritures de Brillat-Savarin
Pot-au-feu Dodin-Bouffant, paré de ses légumes
Purée Soubise
Desserts

Wines: whites: Coteaux de Dézaley, Château-Grillé; reds: Châteauneuf-du-Pape, Ségur, Chambolle.

That was all. The triumph was total. And as a result, Dodin-Bouffant fell in love with his cook. The description of the pot-au-feu is a masterpiece of culinary literature: "The pot-au-feu itself, lightly rubbed with saltpeter and dusted with salt, was cut into slices, and was so fine that the mouth sensed, ahead of time, how deliciously breakable and crumbly this flesh would be. The aroma that emanated from it derived not only from the juices of the beef that steamed forth like incense, but also from the energetic odor of the tarragon with which it was impregnated, and from a very few cubes of transparent, immaculate lard which had been inserted into the meat. The rather thick slices of meat, whose velvetiness was already felt by the lips, rested gently upon a pillow composed of a large slice of sausage chopped up into pieces, the pork being accompanied by the finer flesh of veal, to which was added chopped thyme and chervil. Yet these delicate meats, cooked in the same bouillon as the beef, were themselves supported by an ample carving of chicken wings and breasts, boiled in their broth along with a veal knuckle, rubbed with mint and wild thyme. And to prop up this triple and magic superposition, the fat and robust support of a comfortable layer of fresh foie gras cooked simply in Chambertin had been audaciously slipped behind the white meat of the chicken, which had been fed solely with milk-soaked bread. The alternating disposition of ingredients followed the same order, forming layers clearly demarcated by an envelopment of assorted vegetables cooked in the bouillon and finished in butter."[9] Needless to say, the exaltation of the guests was total, and the meal a far greater success than that of the Prince. Though this was undoubtedly a superb dish, today it would seem as overbearingly complex and heavy as many of the dishes served by the Prince of Eurasia. It is clearly not the pot-au-feu that was to be had, over a half century later, at Léon de Lyon, nor that which is served in thousands of homes every day in France. It remains, however, a highly charged symbolic substitute imbued with domestic love, one whose complexity and perfection in no way detracts from its folkloric nature. Once again, the French earth has the upper hand over a soulless, decadent, suspiciously internationalized cuisine.

Allen S. Weiss

As indicated by the dedication of his book, Marcel Rouff was friends with the greatest gastronome of his time, Curnonsky, "The Prince of Gourmets." Together, they helped establish the discourse of regional French cuisine. While the nineteenth century saw several efforts to establish such regional cuisines in Paris, they met with little success; the most notable example was that of the excellent restaurant Les Frères Provençaux, which soon had to transform its cuisine into a more Parisian model, due to a general lack of interest in their culinary origins. The regionalization of French cuisine had to await not only a reaction against the geographically limited ideals of the bourgeoisie, but also the advent of a more material phenomenon, the automobile. The first *Guide Michelin* published in the year 1900—created to facilitate travel by car (and thus increased the use of tires, Michelin's major product)—was to have an inestimable effect on the history of French cuisine. As automobiles became increasingly comfortable, reliable and fast, the concentric circles around Paris of touristic discovery, culinary and otherwise, rapidly increased. This investigation and celebration of the provinces served not only aesthetic purposes: the culinary symbolism of the French earth was already being placed in the service of a reactionary politics, where even the seeming innocence of Dodin-Bouffant would take on sinister implications in light of the global catastrophe to follow.

In 1913, Marthe Daudet—wife of Léon Daudet, editor of the reactionary journal *L'Action française*—published in Paris, under the pseudonyme Pampille, *Les bons plats de France,* a nostalgic gastronomic incarnation of royalism and Catholicism. This anti-modernist cookbook, a celebration of family values and peasant mores, of rural national cuisine and regional specialties, begins with two recipes: the pot-au-feu and the poule-au-pot. In fact, the entirety of France is divided into four regions, demarcated by the four great national soups: pot-au-feu, onion soup, leek and potato soup, cabbage soup.[10] This reactionary symbolization of the earth and its bounties, of roots, blood and race, was, on the gastronomic level, a direct attack against the French haute cuisine of the great Parisian restaurants and international hotels, a culinary tradition deemed degenerate in its overrefinement and its great distance from the true source of all cuisine, the earth. It should be noted, of course, that this folkloric essentialization of country cooking was a Parisian phenomenon. The semiologist Eugenio Donato explains how, for example, in regard to the 1855 classification of the wines of the Médoc, such essentialization was established, with "the form of metropolitan rationalization being extended to the provincial earth, in the guise of the reflection of an order locked in the earth itself."[11] On the culinary level, the notion that a given wine or dish "cannot travel" assures a certain insularity of the provinces, to remain ever safe from Parisian appropriation. Symbolic closure entails psychological security.

While the automobile permitted the creation of a circuit of culinary discovery that extended from Paris to the provinces, the inverse circuit, from the provinces to Paris, was established by another great technological invention of the century, the radio. In 1928, the gourmet establishment La Maison Corcellet, along with the publisher Flammarion and Radio-Paris, initiated a competition that invited listeners (who were mostly women), to submit their best recipes, thus creating a multi-regional network of culinary informants. The very first prize awarded went to a Madame Paul Julien from Chantilly, for her *ballotine d'agneau Judic,* and the winning recipes were eventually collated in a volume dedicated to regional cuisine. As Alberto Capatti explains, "A major consequence was that female cooks, until then relegated to the second rank by male chefs, by culinographs and by masculine gastronomic clubs, finally had their revenge."[12] Both the geographic and the class circles were closed, and the sundry regional cuisines finally achieved their proper gastronomic status, one which would eventually permit certain female chefs, the famed Mères Lyonnaises, to win Michelin's highest honors. Ironically, a reactionary sensibility would help advance, however slightly, the professional status of women.

A recent poll indicated that 17 percent of the French believe that pork spare-ribs belong in a pot-au-feu. What can this statistic possibly mean, in a postmodern gastronomic context, where new dishes increasingly exist as multiregional and polycultural hybrids, and where culinary authenticity has become a function of an ever mobile and dissatisfied nostalgia, such that tradition itself is continually rehabilitated and recreated? These reflections can be allegorically framed between two dishes. Before enjoying the pot-au-feu at Léon de Lyon, my friend had the bad luck of ordering a first course of a suspiciously pleonastic nature: a *huitre en gelée* (oyster in aspic). The redundancy of jellies—the aspic and the oyster itself—was nearly nauseating. In a similar vein, another dish, glimpsed at a different restaurant, was equally disturbing: a pot-au-feu *en gelée,* a paradoxical, oxymoronic, nonsensical cold-hot-pot. The pot-au-feu, like regional cuisine in general, has for some time been absorbed into the now limitless global network of an haute cuisine in constant flux and hybridization, a state of affairs which, at least in its successful moments, certainly operates to the vast benefit of cuisine. The pot-au-feu has thus been rescued from a sinister symbolic fate. Unfortunately, as recent political discourse has made evident, the earth—despite the best efforts of a few radical Nietzscheans still trying to liberate it—is continually being annexed for the most hideous of motives and the most destructive of politics. If only the joys of cooking could be matched by an equally joyful and liberatory political wisdom.

[This text was initially presented at the colloquium, "Thème de la Flamme," organized by Renaud Camus at the Château de Plieux, May 1997.]

Notes

1. Roland Barthes, "Lecture de Brillat-Savarin," in *Oeuvres complètes* (Paris: Le Seuil, 1996), p. 288.
2. Jean-Anthelme Brillat-Savarin, *Physiologie du goût* (1825; Paris: Flammarion, 1982), pp. 81-82.
3. J.-K. Huysmans, *Là-bas* (Paris: Gallimard/Folio, 1985), back cover.
4. Ibid., p. 84.
5. Ibid., pp. 84-85.
6. Ibid., pp. 85-86.
7. Ibid., p. 89.
8. Ibid., p. 342.
9. Marcel Rouff, *La vie et la passion de Dodin-Bouffant, Gourmet* (1924; Paris: Stock, 1984), pp. 104-105.
10. See Alberto Capatti, chapter on "La croisade des régionalistes," in *Le goût du nouveau* (Paris: Alban Michel, 1989), especially pp. 223-225.
11. Cited in Adam Gopnik, "Is There a Crisis in French Cooking?", *The New Yorker,* April 28 & May 5, 1997, p. 154.
12. Capatti, op. cit., p. 232.

Alphonso Lingis

The Sovereign's Table

astery has been most often conceived in opposition to
hedonism. Asceticism exploits the possibility of mastery over hedonist proclivities; the irradiations of pleasure are open to an inner instance that can control, limit, direct, and eventually extinguish them. Hedonism would result simply from liberation from this instance.

Yet the lifting of this external control does not of itself produce the most intense and the most extensive irradiations of pleasure. To extend pleasure to the broadest ambit requires a positive force which envisions limits and barriers and compulsively transgresses them. To intensify pleasures to incandescence requires a positive force which deepens the abyss under them, compounds them with anguish and repugnance. What gives hedonism its force is the supplement of pleasure, which is the pleasure of power. There is a mastery that produces hedonism and is produced in it.

Gourmandise extends the ambit of its pleasures by curiosity and experiment, intensifies its pleasures by ingenious and recherché combinations and contrasts, sustains its absorption by inventiveness and novelties. Gusanos de manguey, inch-long eel fry, and ants' eggs were the hors d'oeuvres of the best restaurant I ate in in Mexico City, followed by the spiced testicles cut from the bull killed that afternoon in the corrida. An appetite free of prejudices and bigotry, ready to credit the traditions and legacies of cultures across humanity, made of curiosity and the empirical spirit, experimental and inventive, appears to be innocence itself. Sensuality can claim its fundamental innocence and goodness here before attempting to validate sensuality in the hot passions of concupiscence and combativeness and in the cold passions for wealth, power, and glory.

Gourmandise can seem to require nothing more than abandon—to the vital appetites of nature, as well as to the natural inclinations to curiosity and experiment. Moreover, it can seem to rest on an abandon to original, or infantile nature: it would be the adult elaboration of the polymorphously perverse voracity of infancy.

An infant is seen to put anything it touches in its mouth, to taste the maternal breast, its own fingers, the pencil eraser, its doll, jellybeans, marbles, dirt, its pee and poo. Pushing one through childhood consists in fixing on virtually everything within reach taboos against nibbling. Adult gourmandise would honor these taboos in the breach—the *Aufhebung*—maintaining them only as the taboos of hygiene and table manners, while dining on livers, oysters and sea cucumbers.

There is however a limit to appetite: gourmandise is circumscribed by a taboo put on human flesh. The law: eat not of my body, drink not of my flesh is constitutive of gourmandise, not only marking human flesh and blood with abhorrence but driving taste everywhere but there. This law would taboo a return to the original and infantile cannibalism, the oral aggressivity with which the infant draws in the maternal fluids and bites against her flesh.

But is not gourmandise the exercise of a power and a pleasure of power, and therefore adult? Maturity—wealth and power—makes gastronomy possible, extending the array of alimentation beyond what infantile tastes and infantile appetite would cover. Does not this reductionism—explaining and experiencing adult gourmandise as a return to the polymorphously perverse voracity of infancy limited by a taboo maintained on infantile cannibalism—in reality project back upon infancy an adult power structure?

Voracity is universal in nature, in that every living organism eats and drinks, and its flesh is destined to be eaten, its fluids drunk. All living things, however gentle, however rapturously beautiful, however much marvel and adoration they evoke, are in reality segments of a global food chain, where nothing can live without devouring the lives of others, without being destined to feed the appetite of others. As soon as an animal weakens to the point of being unable to run off or kick them off, hyenas and vultures gather about it. As soon as it was born, gnats and flies gathered about it. In the vigor of its life, minute mites are gnawing at its flaking flesh, microorganisms are chewing at whatever it puts in its stomach for its own nourishment.

But an original polymorphous perversity of natural appetite is not the norm. What is instead the norm in the natural world is a specialization of organisms to a small number, or even a single source of alimentation. The finches that had somehow reached the Galapagos and, as Darwin discovered, had mutated into seventeen species, had now as many different diets. Zebras, antelopes, and wildebeests can graze together because they are in fact seeking out different species of plants. The human infant extends its alimentation by overcoming distaste for vegetables, for meat, for lobsters, for frogs, for wine, for cigarettes.

The human animals feels repugnance and horror before a human corpse, the categorical taboo fixing the limits of appetite. But humans, virtually alone among animals, also kill members of their own kind in order to devour them. The taboo is transgressed.

Our most intense horror identifies infantile cannibalism as the original form of cannibalism. Annie Dillard speaks with unrelievable horror of the female wasp which was not able, due to a few days of uninterrupted rain, to find a suitable body of another animal to plant her eggs in, and now those eggs have hatched in her own body and are consuming it from within.

The reductionism is not only found in psychoanalytic but also in folk theory. Parents fantasize the infant, even the foetus, as devouring its mother. According to a very ancient Hungarian folk belief, shamans are born with teeth and bite their mothers' nipples. This same reductionism is reflected in law and public opinion, which penalizes patricide infinitely more severely than infanticide, as though the impulse to commit patricide were especially strong and therefore needed to be curbed by especially violent means.

Statistics, however, ethnopsychiatrist Georges Devereux points out,[1] tell a very different story: throughout the course of history, infinitely more children have been killed either before or after their birth by their parents than parents have been killed by their children. Child sacrifice, too, are much more common than parent sacrifices. The eating of children in times of food shortages is far from rare. But times of famine hardly give us reports of children killing their parents in order to eat them.

Devereux argues that the taboo on cannibalism, and the cannibalistic impulses that it must so categorically prohibit, are specific to adulthood. Adult pedophagic compulsions are the original form of cannibalism. Zoologists understand that the female animals that have just given birth devour the placenta and the cord because they contain certain active substances that help her body achieve the hormonal shift from the pregnant to the lactating state. Lorenz reports mother animals that go on to eat their newborn offspring too. The eating of the afterbirth is not unknown in human cultures. The impulse to go on to devour the infant too is projected onto mythic figures. The infant Dionysus was devoured by the Titans, and would grow up to be a cannibal. Pelops was cooked by his father, and Demeter consumed his shoulder blade. Thyestes ate his children, who had been cooked and served to him. Itys was murdered and cooked by his vindictive mother, Procne, who then fed his flesh to his father, Tereus.

It is never the child, but always the parent who says, "I love you so much I could eat you." Is not the experiencing and explaining of adult cannibalistic impulses as a return to the oral-aggressive impulses of infants a projection on the part of adults? It is the mother that experiences violent and strange oral cravings during pregnancy and upon giving birth; the phantasm of the cannibal infant projects these inward to the voracity of the foetus; the responsibility for the mother's violent oral cravings is attributed to the unborn child. And the parents further suggest cannibalistic behavior to their children—for instance, when they say that certain cookies look like human beings or animals and that it will therefore be fun to eat them.

One eats the cookies—one eats liver, oysters, and sea cucumbers—in order not to eat the children. And in order to not give of one's blood to drink, or one's flesh to eat.

By bringing every plant, every fish, every serpent, every bird, every mammal to the table, we put ourselves at the summit of the great chain of Being.

It is in this way that we posit our value, posit ourselves as values—more exactly, in philosophy's terminology, posit our dignity. Value is the measure of exchange; the value of something is determined by the other things taken to be equivalent to and

Francisco Goya, *Supreme Extravagance,* 1824-1828. Drawing, from the Albums of Bordeaux. Black crayon, 19x15cm. Prado Museum, Madrid.

interchangeable with it. In an economic system, something acquires more and more value in the measure that more and more things are required in exchange for it. Something acquires that transcendent state Kant calls dignity when all things maybe or may have to be exchanged for it, but is not exchanged for anything further. The members of a society exchange goods of necessity with one another, exchange goods and labor for protection, exchange labor and luxuries for temples and monuments, which are not exchanged for anything further; the society will sacrifice its wealth and the lives of its citizens to protect its temples and monuments. In taking possession of jungle and tundra, the oceans and the polar ice-caps, in unhesitatingly defying all the genii loci to make all substances resources for human needs and pleasures, the politico-economic institutions of humankind not only establish their sovereignty within the family of nations, but establish a cosmic sovereignty over all things. In traveling from country to county, being served like the emperor by every alien culture, in restaurants where any substance, any living plant or animal, is laid out for our consumption, we situate ourselves in the food chain at the top, making ourselves the uneaten ones, the unexchangeable value, the cosmic dignity.

But we also eat the cookies—eat liver, oysters, and sea cucumbers—that we induce the children to eat in order to eat the children. To consume the bread they eat and the wine they drink is to consume their flesh and blood.

It was centuries of recurrent famine that put bamboo shoots and seaweed, serpents and sea slugs in the Japanese cuisine. The extension of the Japanese diet is the work of endurance and pride in endurance. To overcome distaste for these things, to extend one's appetite into these dishes, is perhaps the most facile, tourist, way, but also the most substantial way, to accede to this pride. Dining in Mexico City on gusanos de manguey, inch-long eel fry, and ants' eggs, followed by steak cut from the bull killed that afternoon in the corrida, one seats oneself in the ranks of the dominant class, and one also dines with, dines on, the power and pride of the those who endure in the desert and in the corrida.

Notes

1. "The Cannibalistic Impulses of Parents" in Georges Devereux, *Basic Problems of Ethnopsychiatry.* (Chicago: University of Chicago Press, 1980).

Fried Eggs and Soju

he hermit was delighted to see me trudge slowly up the mountain path that wound through the forest past his rustic retreat on Toksung Mountain in South Korea. It was a humid, sunny summer afternoon in 1988, shortly after lunch, and I had decided to slip away from the Buddhist nuns' training temple where I was the only foreigner, and visit an American friend who was living and meditating near to the summit. As a junior nun, I wasn't supposed to be wandering around by myself, but I badly needed a break from the frenetic atmosphere, and I didn't want to ask someone to accompany me. Many of the young nuns still acted like flighty teenagers, and their image of the United States was a bizarre collage of Michael Jackson, Coca-Cola, and the Carpenters.

Leaving the temple, I made my way to the outhouse without exciting suspicion, casually strolled around the back, and then walked quickly away, pausing in the forest to don my overcoat and carefully tie its long sashes into a formal bow. I needed to appear both proper and purposeful, but this was not easy to do. The coat's thin gray polyester fabric, much favored by Korean Buddhist monks and nuns over traditional cotton or linen, was hot and clung unpleasantly to my body. Underneath it I was wearing several more layers, and I felt weak and dazed. Even my feet were coated with a thin, slippery film of sweat in their thin white rubber shoes.

The hermit monk was impossible to ignore. I recognized him from the time I had spent making paper petals for the lotus lanterns for Buddha's Birthday. Appearing in the midst of the junior nuns' work party, he had spent several days strutting about, playing tapes of edifying talks and ogling the young women, who treated him with uneasy deference. He must have had seniority or political clout, as he occupied one of the few hermitages on the mountain. Now he was practically dancing in front of me, torn between joy at my unchaperoned appearance and anxiety that he would blow the whole thing and allow me to get away. I realized that my chances for a cup of tea and comfortable conversation with my American friend had evaporated, and it was time to get real. I'd grown up in a security-oriented middle-class Japanese American family in the rural midwest; I wasn't particularly street-smart. But neither was I an innocent, giggly Korean school-girl.

The hermit monk and I eyed each other warily, and I finally concluded I wasn't clever enough to figure out a way to get past him, but if he tried anything forceful, which I doubted, I was reasonably sure I could kick his ass. He was extremely short and thin, and though horny and conniving, he also looked scared. It probably wasn't every day that he had a chance to fulfill his fantasies.

"Where are you going, Mushim?" the hermit inquired.

"To see the American monk," I answered politely and coolly.

"Why?" he asked.

I couldn't say "None of your business" or "Because I would really like to feel like myself for just half an hour," so I replied, "I need thread." I actually did need some gray thread to mend my clothing, and, like many other small necessities of my daily life, getting it had proven to be exasperatingly difficult for reasons I could not understand. It sounded idiotic to say I was climbing the mountain on a hot afternoon to get some thread, but I couldn't think of anything better, and when questioned in this annoyingly nosy way I was obligated to answer. The young nuns were accustomed to interrogating me fiercely about my activities, and I inevitably attracted a barrage of questions if I even went to the outhouse. I had been physically searched more than once on my way back into the temple, with several of the nuns blocking the doorway and another patting my pockets and around my torso.

"I have plenty of thread!" the hermit said. "Come on in!"

I stalled as long as I could, protesting as vigorously as I could that

I needed to be on my way, but I was only buying time. The hermit monk was banking on the fact that for me to simply walk past him would be inconceivably rude, like blowing one's nose in the middle of a meal or aggressively staring directly into the eyes of one's elder.

"Just a drink of water!" the monk finally insisted. I was hot, thirsty, and stymied. With a sinking feeling, I agreed.

I don't remember the name of that particular hermitage dwelling. There were only three or four on the entire mountain. They were all architecturally distinct, and had their own names and histories of who had lived and practiced at each site. Since some of the materials for the buildings higher up the mountain had to be laboriously hauled by workers, the buildings were all the more precious for the effort that gone into their making. The gentle abbot of the small, exquisite temple at the mountain's summit once told me that he remembered struggling up the rocky path with a loaded wooden A-frame. He had pointed to where the carrying straps had dug into his shoulders, as though the memory caused him pain even after many years.

Pornographic lampoon of a monk. (Probably Paris, 1791).

Although actually only a few feet off the main mountain path, the hermit's dwelling was partially and cleverly concealed from view by a sharp turn in its access path, a copse of trees and a large boulder. A low wooden hand-fashioned gate emphasized the dweller's wish for privacy, and I had gone up only to the gate on previous expeditions with other friends, wondering who lived in the picturesque rustic hut with its high, thatched roof and simple white walls. Set on the side of the forested mountain, it looked exactly like a quaint picturebook illustration of some wonderful cottage inhabited by a sage with a long robe, staff, and long white beard, silently sipping tea and studying calligraphic scrolls. How in the world, I wondered, had this monk, whom I would have placed in the same class as a used-car salesman, landed such a great place to live?

Standing outside the hermitage door, I drank two cups of water and considered what would come next. Unfortunately, by revealing that I was looking for sewing thread I had left myself wide open to having to go inside the hut and politely accept whatever gifts were proffered. I just hoped I didn't get in over my head, and end up in some lurid melodrama, grappling with a sex-crazed monk who was wielding a kitchen knife and trying to rip off my pants. The situation was not without humor, but I wasn't happy about it. I wished fervently that I were back in California, that I were six feet tall, blonde, and had long braids and a Viking sword. I wished that I had studied martial arts techniques and could paralyze opponents with a single touch to the elbow, as I had once heard my *T'ai chi* teacher's teacher could do. I wished I felt assertive and self-confident and healthy instead of numb and suffocated inside heavy layers of polyester. But most of all, I wished I wasn't protein-starved, hungry and thirsty. It weakened my position more than I liked to think.

Even now, sitting in the safety of my Oakland apartment, my husband and son nearby, talking about hunger makes me feel afraid. In America, there's something shameful about hunger because we are surrounded by so much food. We throw away piles and piles of food. We grow fat. To have known hunger seems equivalent to begging on the streets, to being lazy or incompetent or hopelessly dysfunctional. That's not my personal view, but I've learned not to bring up the topic of hunger, or poverty, in any concrete way among middle-class people at social gatherings—it always precipitates a queasy silence, and rarely meets with more than a rote response.

My spiritual training in the United States was about hunger, among other things. In 1985 I was living in a Zen Buddhist temple in Michigan. We were a small, financially-strapped organization, and we usually ate two meals a day, which was somewhat difficult as we worked long hours and followed a strict meditation schedule. During one particularly distressing period our chief cook was a legally-blind teenager who felt he was economizing by purchasing loaves of day-old white bread at the supermarket for 25 cents per loaf. Temple residents who worked outside jobs during the week, myself included, would open our sack lunches, the second and last meal of the day, to find a skimpy, limp tofu sandwich as the main offering, with another sandwich spread with a thin layer of honey as "dessert." (I eventually complained to the resident priest, who simply rolled his eyes and said with admirable humor, "It kind of takes meditation practice into a whole new realm.") We were very far from starving, and prided ourselves on our usually "healthy" diet of rice and vegetables, but after a couple of years I had to admit I was hungry. I realized this when, sitting in a small urban park one day taking my noon break from the law office where I worked as a secretary, I spied a half-eaten cornbeef sandwich poking out of some fairly clean-looking wax paper in a garbage can. Without hesitating I plucked the sandwich out of the garbage and devoured it, discovering a Kosher dill pickle wedged into the corner of the wax paper and scarfing that down as well. It was delicious. I remember sitting in the sun and looking around at the well-dressed office workers around me, then at a group of street people with shopping carts across the street. One of them was an old man with a scruffy beard and only one arm, a well-known town character everyone called Charley. He probably didn't have any inhibitions about eating out of garbage cans either. I wondered what had happened to me.

Food was a matter of utmost importance in the Buddhist monasteries in Korea. For the older generation, memories of starvation and deprivation during the Korean War remained vivid, and in the monastic culture where much of the lifestyle was still intensely physical, eating heartily and keeping up one's strength were primary to survival. In the nuns' temple where I lived, meals and snacks were emotionally charged events surrounded with so many customs and fraught with so much tension that, although I have always loved cooking and eating, I lost my appetite and began to rapidly lose weight. Unlike some other Westerners who attempted to enter the Korean monasteries, I had grown up in a Japanese American family and was accustomed to eating white rice every day. I liked the taste of Korean food well enough. Yet I became drained instead of nourished by the social act of eating, and the exhausting negotiations of giving, receiving, trading, and smuggling food that constantly went on around me, reinforcing bonds between friends of affinity, political allies, and lineage clan members. Toward the end of my time in Korea I was drastically underweight, and quite weak; I no longer like to see zoo animals who pace their cages, leaving well-prepared offerings of fruit or meat untouched. I had never understood so poignantly that a home-cooked meal in one's native country, eaten in peace with family or friends, was a gift to be received with profound gratitude.

However, it wasn't as though I was insensitive to the elegant form and art of eating that I learned during my brief career as a nun in Korea. The monastic-style formal meals, highly choreographed affairs consumed quickly and in silence, typically consisted of fermented bean paste or seaweed and turnip soup, hot white rice, and a small assortment of side dishes of different varieties of *kimch'i,* vegetables pickled in salt and red pepper. Members of the community were served in order of seniority, and special care was taken in laying out particular floor mats and reserving certain small wooden tables for the older nuns; I was once scolded severely while working in the kitchen for mixing up two little tables that looked similar to my untrained eye. Punctuated by the crack of a split bamboo stick *(chukpi)* struck across the palm of the hand to signal the various stages of serving, eating, and clearing away of dishes, meals were consumed using cloth-wrapped sets of wooden or plastic eating bowls. These were rinsed with a small amount of warm water, dried, and reassembled at the end of the meal. Every speck of food in one's bowls had to be consumed, and it was bad form to leave oil streaks or smears of red pepper on one's starched white wiping cloth.

Breakfast, lunch, and dinner were essentially very similar, with lunch being the largest meal, preceded by a quick service in the upstairs Buddha Hall, for which the young nuns donned their formal robes and chanted while prostrating before the figures on the altar. During the service one of the *haengjas,* young women with their heads as yet unshaven who had recently become candidates for ordination, would enter the large, rather chilly room, bearing a footed metal dish that held a perfectly sculpted, breast-shaped mound of freshly cooked white rice. This was placed reverently on the altar as an offering. More than anything else, that daily offering of completely symmetrical, dazzling white rice signified to me that I was participating in a traditional, homogenous culture in which everyone could relate unfailingly and deeply to

A Jesuit Inspects Buttocks of a Urinating Woman. Frcm
*Historiche print en Dicht Tafereelen, van Jan Baptist Girar en
Juffrou Maris Catharina Cadiere* (1735).

the basic and primary food of existence. There was nothing comparable in American culture, where possibly the only foods that bound us together as a nation were burgers and fries. In Korea, even a spoonful of cooked rice was never, ever thrown away, and the correct thing to do if one found a grain of rice sticking to the floor while sweeping or mopping was to immediately pop it into one's mouth.

To be well-fed was to be at home with one's well-being; to be hungry was to be vulnerable, a foreigner, even in one's cwn culture.

I doubt, however, that the hermit saw any of this as he tried to figure out how he could both lay me and guarantee my silence later on. I was by this time seated on the floor of his hermitage hut, which proved to be a lovely and, by Korean standards, fairly spacious room with a tiny kitchen adjoining. The traditional *ondol* floor was covered with clean yellow paper, and *shoji*-type windows allowed natural light softly into the room. On the side of the room facing the windows there were built-in wooden cabinets with sliding doors, and shelves for a ceramic tea set, calligraphy brushes and rice paper, and a few other artifacts. Had I been there with a friend, dressed in American clothing, and with a more congenial host, I would have felt thrilled to be sitting in such an exotic setting, surrounded by green trees on a mountain in Asia where the song of cuckoos echoed through the small canyons.

The hermit monk rummaged around in a cabinet, and produced a cardboard box filled with spools of thread, which he offered to me, waving his hand generously and urging me to take as much as I needed. After I had chosen a couple of spools of light and dark colored thread, he examined me closely and said, "How about an egg?"

Eggs were precious contraband items in the monastic food system, and the only other eggs I'd eaten had been secretly cooked over a tiny backpacker's burner in the room behind the kitchen where the *wonju,* or head cook, lived with her assistant. The *wonju sunim* was my "cousin" in the nuns' lineage families to which we belonged, and she liked to pounce on me whenever I came to the kitchen to get water for drinking or washing my clothes, pull me into her room and feed me Skippy peanut butter on white bread, eggs, oysters, cakes and crackers, and whatever else came her way through the complex exchange of favors that made up the social fabric of the nuns' daily existence. Groaning loudly at my loss of weight, which in America would have enabled me to wear designer clothing and be considered attractive, my cousin would strip down to the man's T-shirt she wore beneath her gray nun's jacket and proudly display her well-developed biceps and solid shoulders. She was always very kind to me and, unlike some of the other young nuns, did not follow her overtures of friendship with sexual advances or attempts to make me perform in amusing ways.

The reality was, I was hungry. I wanted the hermit's food very much. But I had to consider that saying yes to the egg was a seriously unwise concession on my part. Eating food someone has prepared is always an intimate act, even if we've forgotten this is so. It binds us together at the basic level of existence, makes us allies rather than enemies. Consider Persephone, doomed to remain with chill Hades half of each year, because she had thoughtlessly eaten a few pomegranate seeds in the land of the dead. And the hermit monk, also, was hungry, though not for food.

He wasn't an isolated case. As far as I could see, celibacy did not come easily to most members of the monastic order. Among the women, fear of pregnancy kept them pretty much in line, and among the men, the strict schedule of the temple lifestyle and the relative social segregation of women, either nuns or lay, made getting some action difficult, though not impossible. Homosexual activity, though hush-hush, also went on. The entire celibate lifestyle support structure was heavily reinforced by traditional mores and the positive value placed upon a woman's virginity. It was a gigantic and very old enterprise, this containment of the urge to procreate, and it rolled along with a fair amount of success, considering the thousands of people who had chosen this way of life. Of course, from a post-Freudian, Western point of view, there was also a lot of strange behavior, compulsive eating, and abusive treatment that probably could be chalked up to repressed sexuality. In the end, it was simply the way of this particular world, neither good nor bad. It worked better for some than for others, and I had no illusions that I wanted to remain celibate once I returned to the States.

Running into his closet-sized kitchen, from which he could still keep an eye on me, the hermit proceeded to fry a few eggs in a skillet, and put together a tray of the usual *kimch'i* and some crackers to accompany the snack. The tension in the air was mounting rapidly as he sat across the small table from me, watching me eat. We were both keenly aware that the afternoon was growing late, and the time had come for a bold move, one way or the other. And so, after some hesitation the hermit went back into his kitchen and produced a bottle of *soju,* a potent alcoholic beverage made from distilled sweet potatoes or corn, I wasn't sure which. Drinking *soju,* with which I naturally had very little experience, was a little like slugging down grain alcohol or several shots of vodka on a hot day. It could produce almost instant inebriation, followed by a stunning headache. Filling two glasses with the clear liquid, he pushed one across the small table between us toward me.

For once, I saw my cultural role with clarity. This skinny, sharp-faced little monk had hoped that because in some ways I resembled a young, properly-raised Korean girl I could easily be intimidated and overwhelmed. Not so. I was an American, raised on John Wayne, Sheriff Matt Dillon, and Bonanza, and the moment had arrived to knock back the shot of whiskey poured by the sneering, unshaven mercenary in the black shirt, then pull my gun and nail him between the eyes. It was time to drink up and leave.

Looking him squarely in the eye, I picked up the glass of *soju* and gulped it down. It tasted horrible, and instantly made the room tilt, filling me with nausea. I hoped I wouldn't throw up as I wobbled to my feet and headed for the door, whereupon my frantic companion, in a last and desperate attempt to get me to stay, threw open the lower sliding doors of the wall cabinets, revealing a large Goldstar color television. I was astounded. Had he somehow concealed an antenna in the thatching of the roof? He flicked on a channel that was broadcasting Korean disco, and we both gaped at grainy close-ups of purple-skinned Korean girls gyrating in metallic mini-dresses, accompanied by canned disco music.

The hermit quickly shoved past me and stood in the doorway, blocking it. He was shaking all over, carried away with the extreme emotion of the moment.

"Mushim, Mushim!" he shouted

I paused and looked at him. He was the most pathetic would-be seducer I had ever met in my life, but I had to admit he had a lot of spirit. Still, I fervently hoped I would never see him again for the rest of my life.

"One hug," he pleaded. "Just one hug!"

I simply picked him up bodily, threw him aside, and ran out of the cottage and down the mountain. As I recall, I was laughing. I was free, and it was almost time for dinner with the nuns.

Ron Scapp

Eating Up:
Restaurants And Class Identity

Hors d'oeuvre: Historico-Gastronomical Materialism

When I was a child my family rarely ate out, unless it was actually to eat outside, which we did quite often during the summer months. On those occasions my mother would prepare everything indoors and then everyone would feast *al fresco*. I was so unaccustomed to dining at restaurants that the first time I was invited to join my friend's family to eat out, I was embarrassed to discover that we were headed to the family's favorite restaurant and not their backyard.

Restaurants intimidated and confused my family; "eating establishments" were places for people with extra money to spend, having others prepare and serve them their meals. Such exchanges of money for services were reserved for doctors and plumbers, and only after having attempted to care for or repair the problem on our own. Restaurants, therefore, were simultaneously sites of failure and indulgence: who could not or would not cook his or her own meal or desired to be so public about not doing so?

It would not be until I was a teenager and a working musician that eating out became part of my normal social interaction. Though the 1960s were causing social upheavals of all sorts, it was to be my absence from the family's Sunday dinner table which proved most disturbing to my parents. Because I was earning money from my efforts as a musician, however, there was a psycho-economic dynamic at play allowing my absence to be tolerated, if never fully endorsed. Adolescent psychological and artistic successes notwithstanding, questions concerning where and what I ate and how much I spent while at rehearsals or performing remained for quite some time, although more out of curiosity and fascination than anything else. It was within this context of work, family drama and ignorance that my eating at restaurants evolved.

The Charming Hostess:
How to Entertain Economically and Delightfully[1]

The main reason for my parents not entertaining at home had to do with the fact that the apartment we lived in simply did not allow for it. The original dining room was, of necessity, converted into a living room because the living room was needed as a bedroom. The kitchen, large as it was, became the sole location for "dining" and thus entertaining would mean including the children by default. Though my brother, sister and I were willing to stay out of the way, we had no real separate place in our apartment to remain for the duration of a dinner party. Our bedrooms were just off the kitchen and any guests being entertained would disturb us if we tried to sleep and we likewise would disturb them if we ventured out from behind our bedroom doors. Entertaining involved everyone enduring something: the guests had to be mindful of the fact that the children were just within earshot and the children had to behave. Although my parents actually enjoyed their children and liked having us around, even when guests were being served dinner, real entertainment, that is, real parties occurred outside the home; *stepping out* for an adult good time was a given. Thanks to television, however, we did watch other families hold dinner parties and entertain in a fashion that was beyond our means. Like much of the rest of (white) America during the early sixties, we watched the projected image of family life transmitted nightly into our (converted) living room.

These days it appears that many Americans eagerly look outside the home for their dining entertainment. People celebrate birthdays, graduations, promotions and other milestones of their lives in a variety of public places ranging from McDonald's to the most trendy of restaurants. For most Americans, eating out, eating quick and (attempts at) eating cheap are all merged with the act of eating with others, of being with others. When these eating/entertaining dramas unfold in expensive venues, there are

interesting changes in the acts of participation, but being enter-
tained by the staff, the other clientele and by the food itself is
very much part of the dining experience many have come to
expect.

Across America people are still hosting formal dinner parties,
and if the popularity of television's hostess *extraordinaire*
Martha Stewart is any indication, such gatherings are on the
rise. But for many more Americans unable to host wine tastings
in their gardens, restaurants have become the site where indi-
viduals can be entertaining while dining if unable to entertain by
dining. Interestingly, many of the *hoi polloi* have worked their
way into the best of restaurants to have a good time; everyone at
the table, if they are willing (even if unable) to pay for it, can be
a charming host for a moment or two. Restaurants are places

where the social mix can prove to be a surprising cross-class intermingling, and evoke complex tensions as well as pleasures.

Dining with Michael: The (Homo)Erotics of Eating Out

In her book *Epistemology of the Closet*, Eve Kosofsky Sedgwick convincingly argues:

> ...that an understanding of virtually any aspect of modern Western culture must be, not merely incomplete, but damaged in its central substance to the degree that it does not incorporate a critical analysis of modern homo/heterosexual definition; and *[Epistemology of the Closet]* will assume that the appropriate place for that critical analysis to begin is from the relatively decentered perspective of modern gay and antihomophobic theory.[2]

The complex interaction of *men being with men* identified by in her book as "homosocial" (namely, that it is one of the most "natural things" in the world that people of the same gender desire to be together), might well define the structure and character of my dining with Michael. Sedgwick's characterization of the "homosocial" helps, here, to bridge an often overlooked connection between gender and class identity, a connection worth noting between and among men of even marginal or no class differentiation. Through a "homosocialized" mixture of culinary and economic desire Michael introduced me to another level of eating: dining out for the *pleasure* of it.

While the necessities of work, of playing music, led me from my family's kitchen table to the booths, counters and stalls of numerous diners, barbecue spots and other inexpensive restaurants, it was the pleasure of Michael's company, his money and his discerning palate that brought me to the "grand tables" of some of New York's finest chefs. It was with Michael that eating became an event in and for itself—going to a restaurant was something separate from work!

The pleasure of dining with Michael was divided, however unequally, into the sheer delight of his company and the enjoyment of his (relative) wealth. Though growing up in an industrial area of Queens and thus living among the factories, warehouses and workers of the area, Michael had money. Everyone in his family worked and worked very hard, and unlike my fam-

ily, his managed to acquire a level of economic security unattainable by my own hard-working and frugal parents. Coupled with his family's professional relationship to food and dining (his father was at different times a chef and maitre d'), Michael's impulse to be with his male friends gradually moved us off the streets and into restaurants. Suddenly, friends found themselves gathered around a table, arguing about a variety of issues while waiting for more wine to come.

The experience of eating with a friend just for the pleasure of it allowed a number of (repressed) emotions to emerge. On the one hand, there was the recognition of the indulgence of eating at a restaurant without the pretext of "having to do so" because of work; on the other hand, there was the awkward pleasure of enjoying Michael's warmth and generosity: Michael often graciously paid for dinner. The former was not that difficult to acknowledge or accept; one had the right to "indulge" if one could afford it, if one had earned it. But this is precisely what made the latter difficult to accept, even if acknowledged: namely, that my indulgence in eating at restaurants was subsidized by, if not predicated on, Michael's generosity and desire. Just as being served was always a complicated and difficult experience (despite my paying for the privilege), being "treated to dinner" was, in many ways, even more problematic.

"Dining out" was always done self-consciously, that is, being served was offset by the knowledge that I was responsibly staying within my limits. But Michael's desire took me well beyond those limits. He would often absorb the cost of my transgression with a welcoming smile—we would have many such dinner dates. At one point, we would "go out" once a week somewhere to enjoy a meal and each other.

He took particular delight in our dinner dates, partly because he was simply generous and partly because of the pleasure he derived from supporting his "socialist" friend with money from stock dividends his family earned from shrewd investments ("tips" his father got from customers). In Michael one saw the benevolent and attractive face capitalism now and again puts forth, however temporarily and naively. His love, warmth and friendship seduced me, allowing me to eat at places I never considered before and for no other reason than the pleasure of it.

Aiming for the Stars

Of all my dining experiences, none is more memorable than the first time I ate at a bona fide three-star restaurant. Despite my learned comfort with eating at expensive restaurants in New York and other cities throughout the United States, nothing had prepared me for my first time in a European three-star restaurant. All my "eating up" had me convinced that I could not, would not, be intimidated, overly impressed or made to feel awkward by the "stars" themselves: class was no longer the issue, just the food and the eating experience itself.

Of course, I had never seriously considered the possibility of falling prey to the class equivalent of "backsliding," of lapsing back into a previously bad state of affairs, in this case of being profoundly aware of my class status or lack thereof. The moment I entered the now defunct Gualtiero Marchesi of Milan, I reentered an emotional realm of my youth, of my historical uneasiness with such things as being served, with spending hundreds of dollars on a meal!

Horseback Dinner at Sherry's Restaurant. New York, 1903. Photograph by Byron

Suddenly everything was difficult: too many glasses, utensils, and waiters. Choices needed to be made that would determine the outcome of the entire dining extravaganza and I was somewhere else, somebody else. It was a moment of opposite force to the Heideggerian anxiety of pondering "from whence we come?" I knew too well from whence I came; the issue was: could anyone tell? The re-inscription of class anxiety, of questioning one's worth and value and of projecting significance elsewhere, that is to say "up there," is often automatic and involuntary. Like entering a room and detecting an aroma that throws you back in time, encountering the signs of traditional class privilege and power can push you back. Where? It depends, but often it's back somewhere without clout and immediate legitimacy, somewhere lacking, somewhere certainly that did not allow you to be comfortable among the trappings of opulence.

The food is eaten, the wine drunk, however, and you are transported, for a time, to a place of ethereal splendor. Despite an oscillating consciousness of metaphysical tensions rooted in class identity, the meal, that is, the great meal seduces you back into the pleasures of varied tastes, aromas, textures and colors, seduces you back from any question concerning your desire. You are liberated not by the sway of powerful philosophical concepts that assist you in reconceiving your place in the universe, but are set free by virtue of your very place at the table, sipping your *barbaresco,* swallowing a mouthful of *porcini risotto,* and quietly communicating the joy of the moment to your culinary interlocutors who begin to speak a language whose syntax is primordial and unfixed. Moans of delight and the smacking of lips are ordered and reordered, sounded and resounded neither by logic nor convention, but by the immediate and uncensured response to the meal itself, to the intensity that eating can engender. You are, if not in heaven, certainly among the stars.

In short, you are attended to as never before and the restiveness of your being is quieted by the relaxation that comes from being full, if not quite fulfilled. The cumbersome gestures that were made at the start of this journey are transformed into the self-assured elegant ones one makes with success, indicating the achievement of aiming high, of aiming for the stars and making it. Some people arrive already having achieved this stature of *being-in-the-world* by dint of their pedigree—the experience is anticipated and repeated, sometimes with the ennui that often accompanies presumption. But for many others, the moment is as unexpected as it is temporary. You have consumed your way to new heights and, as you ascend, questions immediately arise about both the process and content of your consumption. You sigh: something will always be pleasurable and uncomfortable about all of this.

Digestif: Eating (It All) Up

Throughout the world the contradictions of capitalism manifest themselves daily, but perhaps no more strikingly than the extremes that can be encountered through eating and starving. As United Nation officials leave the strenuous debates of the day behind them to dine at the finest restaurants in New York, Paris, Geneva, Brussels and elsewhere, millions suffer from the malnutrition inflicted upon them by the trade and labor agreements achieved by consensus of participating countries. Eventually, we are told, the global economy will find its natural balance. Everyone will enjoy a better standard of living, everyone will be part of the future. But as some await the millennium, eating it all up, others only fear what will be served to them next.

British Army maneuvers.

Eating is foremost about survival, but often it's about living well and pleasure; "eating up" is about political mobility, power and identity. "Eating up" by necessity comes only after "eating" as such, but it comes no less meaningfully or forcefully. "You are what you eat (up)" is the maxim that guides the lives of many these days. The complicated acts of consumption and resulting pleasures that constitute who we are (*who* and *what* we eat up), demand that we begin to consider eating practices on all fronts. The "simple" act of going to a restaurant involves a social-political context we normally ignore in favor of the pleasures of eating itself. Yet, one need not wait to be seated for too long before that social-political context begins to make itself manifest. Restaurants may not be *the* site(s) of metaphysical direction for a given culture, but it is clear that they are places where the *telos* of those individuals who are attempting to eat their way up toward meaning can be witnessed hovering just above the aromas of the Special of the Day.

Notes

1. The title of this section comes from a monograph of the same title written by Gloria Goddard for the series "Little Blue Book" (Number 1209) edited and published by E. Haldeman-Julius. Such booklets on etiquette can be found from the late 1800s onward and provide the reader with abridged guidelines to social class and character.

2. Eve Kosofsky Sedgwick, *Epistemology of the Closet* (Berkeley: University of California Press, 1990).

Gregory Whitehead

Chowderhead

I'm way down harbor in my kayak, too far, really, but home-ward bound against a light breeze. Suddenly the fog rolls in from nowhere, the temperature drops fourteen degrees in three minutes, the mercury registers in every bone. There I float in a salty stupor, can't even see the end of my paddle. My shoulders hurt, my head hurts, my fingers would hurt if they weren't so numb. Damn.

What I need is a big bowl of chowder.

Fortunately, I don't even have to pull out the compass, for my stomach is already on automatic pilot, drawn by gastromagnetism to the most restorative eatery I have ever chanced to discover, a place where the notion of Bed & Breakfast has long been supplanted by the infinitely more compelling duet of a wicked cuppachowdah followed by a hard, deep sleep—the obscure little Nantucket Inn that, though officially unnamed, has been known since the Age of Ahab as The Try Pots. Tucked away on a small side street in the north of town, far from the ruts and hungers of pasty daytrippers and red-panted "yaughties," two enormous black wooden pots swing from the crosstrees of an old topmast, with the horns sawed off on the far side, such that this pickled mast resembles a brig's gallows, still very much in use.

A peculiar sign, and one that well reflects the richly inflected humors of the current proprietors, Laura and Josiah Hussey, whose devotion to the island of Nantucket, through all the writhings of her present plunder, is only surpassed by their passionate commitment to ladling out steaming portions of their family tradition, a glorious five-generation legacy served up in a bowl. Though their chowder may not change the course of Nantucket history, it sure does ease the pain.

As always, Josiah greets me at the door, and steers my hurting bones over to a long wooden table whose occupants methodically lift oversized pewter spoons to their lips, the only sound an odd froglike chorus of guttural slurps, punctuated by the occasional highly pitched grunt, an ensemble that gives convincing proof of immeasurable gastronomic contentment. No one takes notice of my arrival. The collective focus is fixed exactly where it should be, on the home-kilned bowls now being rhythmically drained of their generous portions of steaming satisfaction, the last precious morsels mopped up with hunks torn from Josiah's justly famous thick-crust sourdough bread, all chased by frosted glasses of dense, local, Cisco Porter.

I'm home.

Any chowderhouse will exude the briny aromas of the sea, but in the person of Josiah Hussey you will engage an unexpected counterpoint. With a carriage and demeanor that speaks of long hard work in sandy soil, Josiah hails from farm country, Polpis (on Nantucket, if you want to call someone a hick, you say they are "a little Polpisy"). It is he who reminded me several years ago that chowder is not just another name for fish soup, but a dish that aims for a deeper, more complex synthesis between sea (quahogs, cod, scallops, clams, crab, eel, and whatever) and garden (potatoes, onion, pork, and cream). Josiah's an island farmer, then, who does not try to resist the little bit of ocean that is always tiding up his nose. In the Hussey Farm tradition, he feeds both their cows and their pigs on fishmeal and cod parts, and I swear I once saw (as others have sworn to have seen), one big old sow tromping along by the nearby cranberry bog with each foot stuck in a cod's decapitated head, grinding surf into turf. Though I've not witnessed it myself, Laura tells me that Josiah also irrigates their vegetables with water siphoned from kettle drums encrusted with scallop shells, to enhance his chances of achieving the ideal infusion of bay into soil. As he has often said: "It's no secret what we do—soonah or latah, it's all gonna come out in the chowdah."

On this day, like so many others, we don't have to say anything—Josiah knows why I'm here. Laura waves hello from the open kitchen, which is really nothing more than a long, well-seasoned chopping surface in front of a an old Vulcan stove firing up

six huge black metal pots, shaped just like the two wooden icons
that swing from the gallows outside. Six subtle variations on a
strong and soulful melody: "Cod, Clam, Crab, Scallop, Seascape
or Lobstah?", she asks. Though tempted by the Seascape (which
directs a little bit of everything into a grand guignol of roots,
tubers, molluscs, bivalves, gaggers, barnacles and gadiformes),
on this occasion I crave the Cod, straight up.

If Josiah brings a little taste of the ocean into the earth, it is
Laura who knows the secret of giving legs to the sea. She wears
a necklace of codfish vertebrae, inherited from Josiah's great-
grandmother, her ears are studded with matte black pearls, and
her every motion communicates pure mastery over this most
savory art of culinary mixage.

I have often engaged the Husseys on the subject of chowder phi-
losophy, which I quickly learned had nothing to do with the end-

A deckhand aboard the *Ver* poses with a cod. National Museum of Iceland, Reykjavík.

ATTRIBUTS DE COMMERCE

less refinement of set recipes. Both Laura and Josiah prefer to talk about certain fundamental "buoys" that help the cook to navigate, though every new potful is charted afresh.

I: Taste cooked begins with life, raw. Nowadays, most master chefs place tremendous emphasis on the provenance and quality of their materials, but the Husseys take such elemental respect one step further than most, and can tell you in elaborate detail how to store and refrigerate nine different species of shell-fish, in accordance with the specific elements of their natural habitat. Most of their ingredients are alive (or, well, half-alive), until they hit the scalding bottom of the pot. This holds true for vegetables as well as fish; the root cellar at The Try Pots looks like the laboratory of a hyperactive field botanist. A related axiom states plainly: never try to cook what you don't have.

II: Flavor is best released close to the hand. Mechanical food processors are summarily excluded from the Try Pot kitchen, on the grounds that such tools defeat accumulated experience of hand-to-eye. Laura has often demonstrated to me the slight shifts in knife location that will release ranges of juices and flavors that would be lost in the undifferentiated grids of the Cuisinart. Though particularly apt with regards to molluscs and cephalopods, this holds true even for the humble onion. Similarly, sea salt crystals and whole peppercorns are freshly ground, cracked in the largest mortar and pestle I have ever seen.

III: The pig jumps in, out, and in again. Whereas some chowderphiles go so far as to challenge the very presence of the pig, at The Try Pots, emphasis is placed on the porker's movement throughout the cooking process. Laura first browns the finely chopped rasher in the cooking oil (no, not butter, oil: hand-pressed olive and hints of walnut oils used chez Hussey, a faint dribble of heresy), at the onset of each new pot, but then removes it before adding the other ingredients. The browned bits are then added back to each bowl directly prior to serving, adding a crisp and articulate reminder that a sound chowder roams that tantalizing border between land and sea.

IV: Don't rush the cream. At The Try Pots, a pitcher of fresh cream (milked from the Hussey's cod-fed cow, a gentle beast named Foley) is always kept on the table for patrons to add a splash or two themselves, as desired. The Hussey view is that if they succeed in the kitchen, the pitcher will still be mostly full at the end of the day. They believe that most chowder makers routinely over-cream as compensation for their failure to "milk" the ingredients of their own rich and varied juices.

V: Anything goes. For all their magnificent accomplishments, Laura and Josiah remain committed to chowder as an open-pot concept, ever available to improvisation. Inside the Whitehead kitchen, we have often shared our own attempts to "push the rim" with the Husseys, with whom we are fortunate enough to be neighbors. (My own special area of research is the crab, in affiliation with Nantucket corn, whereas Lillian has given center

stage to the oft-overlooked yet immensely flavorful Octopus.)
The discussion usually evolves into minute detail with regards to
culinary technique, but no chowder is ruled out of bounds.
Indeed, I once added a quick shot of port to a bowl of Chowder
à la Venus Mercenaria right in front of Josiah's nose, and he did-
n't bat an eye. And Laura loves to tell the story of her ancestral
cousin, Elijah Starbuck, who logged the emergency ingestion of
an albatross chowder while on a whaling voyage, around Cape
Horn.

So much for soul-saving buoys. Time to eat. Nothing to look at
but the six black pots and the strange swirling design on the wall
at the far end of the kitchen, a design that Laura insists derives
from the tattooed skin of a Polynesian harpooneer who used to
"chowder down" right here at this table.

As I mopped the last bit from the bottom of the bowl, I noted
that the fog was starting to lift, though harbor horns continued
to blast from time to time. For day-trippers, fog is an unwelcome
impediment to their Nantucket dream holiday of maximum solar
radiation; for those who live here, it is a fundamental force of
nature, one that ridicules resistance. Better to welcome the
rolling mists as an excuse to head for the sign of the hanging
black pots, reserved for those hardcore chowderheads who nav-
igate by way of a nose in the air and a hunger that tugs from the
bones.

Stuff

A performance by Coco Fusco and Nao Bustamante

*I*n 1996, we decided to create a performance that dealt with Latin women, food and sex. We started from our own stories.

Nao is from an immigrant farm worker family that was involved in the Chicano political struggles of the 1960s and 1970s. She grew up in the San Joaquin Valley of California, a region that at one time produced more fruit and vegetables than any other in the world. Coco's family is from Cuba, a country that gained a reputation in the 1950s as an international whore-house, and which, in response to its present economic crisis, has reverted to sex tourism as a strategy of survival. In the course of writing STUFF Coco traveled to Cuba to interview women in this burgeoning industry. Then we both went to Chiapas, the center of indigenist culture tourism in Mexico, and the site of the 1994 Zapatista insurrection. We spent several weeks in conversation with women and children whose livelihoods are linked to their daily contact with foreigners.

STUFF is our look at the cultural myths that link Latin women and food to the erotic in the Western popular imagination. We weave our way through multi-lingual sex guides, fast food menus, bawdy border humor, and much more. In the course of the performance, we mingle with audience members, treating them to a meal, a host of rituals and exotic legends, an occasional rumba and at least one Spanish lesson as part of our satirical look at relations between North and South. Our spoof, however, is not without a serious side. Latin American literature is full of references to cannibalism—as the European colonial's fear of the indigenous "other" as a cannibal, as a trope for Europe and America's ravaging of Latin America's resources, and finally, as the symbolic revenge of the colonized who feed off the colonial. If food here serves as a metaphor for sex, then eating represents consumption in its crudest form. We are dealing with how cultural consumption in our current moment involves the trafficking of that which is most dear to us all—our identities, our myths and our bodies. STUFF is our commentary on how globalization and its accompanying versions of "cultural tourism" are actually affecting women of color both in the third world and in Europe and North America, where hundreds of thousands of Latin women are currently migrating to satisfy consumer desires for "a bit of the other."

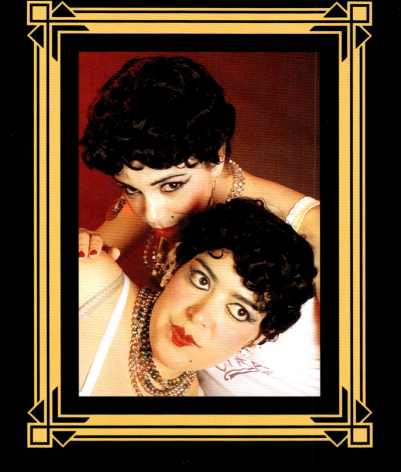

Paquita y Chata Se Arrebatan

un foto-ensayito de Coco Fusco y Nao Bustamante

chismean...

chambean...

se quieren...

sueñan...

tentan...

ceden...

...y gozan.

William PopeL., *Black Cheesecake*, 1997. Peanut butter, *Ebony* magazine clipping on paper, 10 x 7 in.

William PopeL., *Blackhead #1*, 1992. Acrylic paint on frozen pizza, 10 in. diameter.

William PopeL., *Fido Remembers*, 1992. Bag of dog biscuits, *Ebony* magazine clipping, acrylic, 16 x 8 in. Detail.

VIRTUAL GOURMANDISE

Lisbon still possesses the
orange tree from which all those
which embellish and perfume the gar-
dens of Europe originated, for we owe to
the Portugese the very first seeds of that tree
that originally came from China. They trans-
formed the Iles d'Hyères into a new garden of the
Hesperides. I tread upon the orange peels and the oys-
ter shells that evoke the immensity of the seas, and I
simultaneously experience a double joy at a place not
lashed by the waves of the ocean, at a place distant from
the rays that ripen the beautiful yellow fruit.

Louis Sebastien Mercier
The New Paris

Jean-Claude Bonnet

Carême, or the Last Sparks of Decorative Cuisine

"Amidst the prodigal feats of the Directoire, Carême prepared the delicate luxury and exquisite sensuality of the Empire."
A. Dumas, Le Grand Dictionnaire de Cuisine.

The early nineteenth century is a sumptuous era in culinary tradition. While the nineteenth century *mangeur,* to borrow Jean-Paul Aron's term, is very clearly bourgeois, we might do better to forego the moral image of a class that stuffs itself, as it appears in the writings of Grandville, and ask ourselves why gastronomy established itself as a specifically bourgeois cultural discipline at that moment. The revolution had overturned customs and set in motion a cultural transformation that did not spare the realm of the table. With fear now past, one witnessed a culinary restoration. From the Directoire to the July Monarchy, a new appetite emerged, all the more strongly as it was the sign of social affirmation after the frustration of the revolutionary period. Since the eighteenth century, on the other hand, with the *Encyclopédie,* the creation of natural sciences and the birth of biology, nutrition and its problems had been the object of a constant written appraisal. The nineteenth century bourgeois, in his concern for his body, defined the written rules of good breeding and self-control that later became standardized. A great number of books devoted to food appeared at the beginning of the nineteenth century. Among the chorus of culinographers and *gastrolastres,* Carême occupies a very special place. His is the work of an honest craftsman, neither gourmet nor glutton, who speaks of cooking and the status of the cook from the point of view of a practitioner, without literary effects. Carême is, however, an interesting figure of the Empire and the Restoration. At once nostalgic and innovative, he is both the last *ancien régime* style *officier de bouche[1]* and the first artistic chef of bourgeois culture. His obsession with decoration and his passion for drawing are very characteristic of the culture and sensibility of an epoch.

Carême's work is inseparable from the flowering of culinary lit-
erature at the beginning of the nineteenth century, where two
authors in particular stand out. Grimod de La Reynière, during
the Empire, founded a tradition of gourmand writing character-
ized by an artistic, excessive metaphoricality and defined the
gastronomical ritual: tasting committees, prize-lists and nutri-
tive itineraries. With the *Almanach des Gourmands* (1803-
1812), the first gastronomical chronicle written from the point
of view of the host and the gourmet appeared. In *Le Manuel des
Amphitryons* (1808), Grimod, with a certain aristocratic dis-
dain, lays down the ancien régime rules of good manners for the
new eating society. His work is entirely taken up with the eigh-
teenth century nostalgia for ostentation and the certitude that a
new order of things had been definitively imposed. *La
Physiologie du Goût* by Brillat-Savarin (1825), quite unjustly
better known than Grimod's work, is written in an elegant "pro-
fessorial" style. Gastronomy here is not a pretext for brilliant
aesthetic discourse, but becomes a general topic that touches
upon all the sciences, in keeping with a pure encyclopedic tra-
dition. Brillat-Savarin is interested in food from the standpoint
of history, geography, morality, etc. One is as likely to find
Grimod's use of metaphor as Brillat-Savarin's knowledge in a
variety of second-tier texts that make up a significant group. In
La Gastronomie (1802), in four songs in the genre of didactic
poetry, Berchoux proposes a complete course. Presenting him-
self as the Delille of the dinner table,[2] he writes a succinct histo-
ry of cooking and fills his, in alexandrine verses, with precon-
ceived ideas on the art of eating by invoking Apicius and Vatel,
Martial and Plutarch, Rousseau and Legrand d'Aussy. This
rhymed hodgepodge, whose success is attested to by the many
reprintings, well demonstrates the popularity of gourmand writ-
ings. Colnet, in *L'Art de Dîner en Ville* (1810), revives a seven-
teenth and eighteenth century satiric tradition, based on the
topos of the parasite. He explains to the "men of letters" how to
have the rich feed them and writes a history of the eighteenth
century hospitable houses (La Popelinière, Beaujon) and salons
(Mme Geoffrin, Mlle de Lespinasse). In *L'Art Culinaire* (1844),
the marquis de Cussy collects precious gourmet notes, and is
similarly haunted by the eighteenth century. Cadet de
Gassicourt presents *Le Cours Gastronomique* or *Les Dîners de
Manant-Ville* (1809), as "an anecdotal, philosophical and liter-
ary work" dedicated to the Epicurean society *Le Caveau mod-
erne*.[3] Using fiction, he creates the character of the parvenu and

Hermitage russe.

his son instructed by the "phago-technician, Victor Phage," who prefigures Dodin Bouffant. All these works define an atmosphere and mark the stirrings of a new sociality. In them, gastronomy constitutes itself as a national culture on the basis of literary works. Carême's point of view is a different one.[4]

Carême recognizes, in *L'Art de la Cuisine Française* au XIXeme siècle, the inseparable links between literature and gastronomy ("the man of letters knows how to enjoy the pleasures of gastronomy"), but in his preface to the *Cuisinier Parisien* he claims the technical language of cooking for himself alone: "No sensible man can deny the fact that all the arts and trades have their own languages; the man who writes about a craft he does not know makes a fool of himself in the eyes of the practitioners." While the literary gourmands have a certain kind of competence in speaking about cooking, they do nothing for the art's development: "Grimod... has no doubt done some good for culinary Science, but he counts for nothing in the rapid progress that modern cooking has made since the renaissance of the art... It is to the great dinners given by the Prince de Talleyrand during his ministry of foreign affairs and to the famous Robert that we owe the growth of modern cuisine, and not to the author of the *Almanach des Gourmands.*" A. Viard, who, in *Le Cuisinier Impérial* (1814), presents himself as an *homme de bouche,* dissociates himself in similar fashion from gourmand writings: "Let us pay tribute once again to the cult of Comus, and since the poets, literary men and even the scholars do not deign celebrate gourmandism today, or enlist under the tranquil banners of Epicureanism, let us not imagine we are departing from philosophy in publishing a culinary code. Our song-writers can make succulent couplets on this art, the prose-writers can write on this inexhaustible subject; but what can they say that is worth the precise rules followed by an adept, and which are the true poetics of culinary arts?" Carême is equally removed from the stereotyped manuals that tell how to eat on a shoestring. He strives toward "a more honorable endeavor... than *boeuf à la mode*" and calls the new books such as *Le Cuisinier des Cuisiniers,* or *La Cusinière Cordon Bleu,* "puny productions that are far from summarizing great French cooking." The practitioners he refers to are the artists who founded the gastronomical tradition, his colleagues from the late eighteenth century (Iliot, Dalège, Lefèvre) and the early of the nineteenth century (Robert, Laguipière, Lasne).

In the conception of his books, Carême nonetheless has a fair amount in common with the culinary literati on many points. As with them, his discussion of cuisine rests on a foundation of encyclopedic knowledge. He has a library and uses, in the parallel drawn between the *ancien régime* and modern cuisine in his *Maître d'hôtel Français,* Vincent La Chapelle and Iliot, Louis XV's *contrôleur.* As an historian, he specifies, in this same work,

Ruine d'Athènes.

that the seventeenth century's potage (soup) was really a ragoût (stew), and that ouille corresponds to our potage. In *L'Art de la Cuisine Française au XIXeme siècle,* in which he writes a history of cooking, he cites works that constitute a vulgate of gastronomical knowledge: the luxurious feast of Dinias in the chapter "Festins des Grecs" (Greek Banquets) in the *Voyage du Jeune Anacharsis en Grèce* (Voyage of the young Anacharsis in

Greece) by l'abbé Barthélémy; the chapter "Festins des Gaulois"
(Feasts of the Gauls) in *L'Histoire de la Vie Privée des Français*
(History of Private Lives in France) by Legrand d'Aussy; and the
French translations of the *Odyssey* by Mme Dacier. According to
A. Dumas, Carême "wrote and illustrated a history of the Roman
table," of which both text and illustrations have been lost. In a
spirit of "analysis" very close to that of Brillat-Savarin, Carême
refers at once to philosophers such as Cabanis, to ancient dietet-
ic treatises, and to tales of travel. He contributes directly to the
gourmand literature with his "Aphorisms," in which, in the style
of a *grand siècle* moralist, he writes moral and historical banal-
ities on eating. Nonetheless, his writing preserves the serious
tone of an honest craftsman.

Retracing his arduous ascension as an autodidact,[5] Carême
clearly demonstrates that his work is not the babbling of a
gourmet, but rather the product of labor and merit. According to
the marquis de Cussy, "Carême ate very little and did not drink,"
(*l'Art Culinaire,* chap. IX) which is to say he did not share the
gourmand's euphoria. His work does not have the verve or the
metaphorical subtlety of those who consume. It is written from
the point of view of practice: "I had the excellent custom of not-
ing, when I returned home in the evenings, the modifications I
had made in my work, to which each day brought new changes...
These books are my life's thoughts. They represent so many new
pains, preoccupations and worries, and how I tormented by
body and mind with sleepless nights! At daybreak I was at the
marketplace..." ("Une page des *Mémoires de Carême,*" in *Les
Classiques de la table* by Justin Améro, 1855). By giving us the
portraits of the great chefs he knew in the frontspieces of his
works, Carême places them in the context of austere artistic
endeavor. The names of his recipes clearly demonstrate his
desire not to deviate linguistically and to adopt a serious tone.
Cussy notes that Carême "lavished his soups with great names,"
and cites a few of them: "Soups named for Condé, Boïeldieu,
Broussais, Roques, Ségalas (scholars and amiable doctors);
Lamartine, Dumesnil (the historian), Buffon, Girodet, and, to be
fair to everyone, this great practitioner lost to the culinary arts
did not forget to name one of his best soups for Victor Hugo
before he died..." (*L'Art Culinaire,* chap. II). To sign his culinary
creations, the artist uses famous names according to the tradi-
tion of the *ancien régime*: "The dishes of French cuisine bear
the names of the most illustrious members of the French nobil-
ity: *à la reine, à la dauphine, à la royale, à la d'Artois, à la
Xavier, à la Condé, à la d'Orléans, à la Chartres, à la
Penthièvre, à la Soubise,* etc." (*Le Cuisinier Parisien,* p. 12). In

the menu, the names also must make an impression: they must be decorative. In the name of taste, Carême criticizes the "barbarous" terms Menon uses in *Les Soupers de la Cour* (1755): "However, I do not like the name of the entrée he names *les semelles de faisan à la Conti* (pheasant soles à la Conti). I am always surprised that people who make their productions a point of honor to their positions are not more careful in their choices of names, especially in gastronomical sciences; nonetheless, a modern author, a gourmand literary man, noted in his menus an entrée of *filets de boeuf*, sautéed *en talons de botte glacée* (in frozen boot heels); he should have added *cirée* (polished). He certainly is an ingenious fellow to have put beef tenderloin in boot heels and fillet of pheasant into shoe-soles! The two ideas are in the best of taste: one can see that the modern author was inspired by the author of the previous century. He even writes *potage à la jambe de bois* (wooden leg soup) so as not to write *à la moelle* (marrow bone)... and if we add the *culottes de boeuf* (beef's bloomers) and the *veau roulé en crotte d'âne* (veal rolled in ass's dung) from the Cuisinier Gascon, the *culs d'artichauts* (artichoke's bottoms), the *pets de nonne glacés* (glazed nun's farts); then, at table, when one asks the maître d'hôtel what this entrée is...; it becomes even more sensitive when a pretty woman herself is doing the honors of her table, to whom the guest asks the names of the dishes" (*Le Maître d'hôtel Français*, p. 42). The coarse language of the kitchen should be banned from menus. One must sacrifice nun's farts and all the metaphorical language that since the Middle Ages has associated food with debauchery. For Grimod, baptizing dishes is an important moment in gourmand writing, and he does not concern himself with decency, since for him gastronomy is linked to a mythology of pleasure. Carême rejects any search for transgressive language. The great names he gives to dishes "characterizes them in a particular manner," which is to say it integrates them into the decor, the ornamentation, and preserves the homogeneity of the ceremonial. They are hommages paid to great figures, scholars and artists through food. Carême chose the names for his dishes in reference to the culture of his time, so that the wording of a menu would be a delicate combination producing elegant surprises. These names are therefore never incongruous, but rather harmonious. They ring no false notes in the progression of the meal and are on a par with Carême's own virtue. Censuring the frivolity of the names from the *ancien régime,* they mark the advent of the bourgeois meal and reflect the image of Empire and Restoration society back upon itself, unpolished and silent.

It is as a practitioner that Carême broaches the questions untouched by the culinary literati, such as the definition of a new cuisine and a new status for the chef. On his own account, he continues the chef Robert's late seventeenth-century critique of spices. In *Le Maître d'hôtel Français* he indicates that French cooking has been slowly de-Italianizing itself since the Renaissance. The progress goes in the direction of a simplification of the national taste. French cooking should be simpler, more "unctuous" and correspond to "the sweetness of the clear sky and our happy climate." *In L'Art de la Cuisine Française au XIXeme siècle* (p. 62), Carême notes that "ginger, coriander and vanilla were often used in the *ancien régime's* cuisine, while in modern cooking we use them infrequently, or better yet, not at all." Similarly, Cadet de Gassincourt speaks out against hotchpotches and spices. The idea was to isolate and classify flavors, give order to the diversity of tastes; but with Carême the dominant criteria is of an aesthetic order. The artist should play upon the basic flavor, and refrain from seeking sophisticated relationships. The new cuisine is also "less costly" because it abandons the former spatial profusion of tables in favor of a more linear order: "Why not cease this habit of covering bourgeois tables in the manner of the nobles... I propose to serve four dishes instead of eight, and to serve them one after the other" (*L'Art de la Cuisine Française*, p. 59). With all this effort to simplify, Carême founded the bourgeois cuisine of the nineteenth century.

In his effort to define the new role of the chef, Carême is haunted by the ancien régime. In this respect, he appears as a transitional figure. The revolution, in breaking up the old houses, forced the former chefs to open restaurants. In *L'Art du Cuisinier of 1806*, Beauvilliers introduces himself as follows: "Former Officer of Monsieur, Count of Provence, attaché of the gala events of the Royal Houses, and currently restaurant-keeper, rue de Richelieu, no. 26, at the great tavern of London." Carême rejects the mercantile restaurant that breaks the ancient rite of the table and forces chefs to work with "kitchen maids." He wanted the former organizations of houses to be restored at the time when Napoleon, in the imperial palace etiquette of 1808, prescribed the exact same ordinances as Louis XIV for table service. The Emperor has his *nef* and his *cadenas*.[6] The chief marshal of the palace, the prefect and the pages reproduced the same arrangement as before, "the usher, the wine server, the general controller," etc.[7] Carême had read Audiger and d'Arclais de Montamy, who describe the rules of procedure in *ancien régime* houses. He reasserted the former status of the *maître d'hôtel,* or house steward (one of his books from 1822 is entitled, in fact, *Le Maître d'hôtel Français*), which involved a function that goes beyond the simple kitchen: the *officiers de bouche* were the stewards of the house.⁸ In modern houses, on the other hand, everything was "confusion." The traditional hierarchy and the division of labor between the *chef d'office,* the *chef de cuisine* and the *maître d'hôtel* were often forgotten. The *cuisinier* (the chef, or man of great repute) must, according to

Carême, be at the head of a great household. Under Louis XV the culinary artists had the responsibilities of administrators and were treated like nobles: "the extreme good breeding of the court of Louis XV singularly influenced the civilization of all classes of society, but especially the *hommes de bouche,* who, at this time, were justly considered nobles: furthermore, there was not a single lord's chef who did not himself have the bearing and the manners of a man of good breeding: an embroidered suit, lace cuffs and diamond buckles were their garb; the sword was their arm and they knew how to use it." (*Le Pâtissier National,* 3rd part, p. 292). One finds similar nostalgia with Lady Morgan who, reporting an interview with Carême, compares herself to Mme de Sévigné speaking to Vatel. In his desire to earn "the respect of the nobles," Carême seemed like a thin-skinned flunkey. He left some places impulsively because he felt he had not been given his due. Upon his arrival in Moscow, in the service of the Emperor, he remarks that the place of the *maître d'hôtel* has been "debased" and left forthwith, since he had come "to serve the Emperor without surveillance" and because he "could not tolerate this changed condition." At the Princess de Bagration's house, on the other hand, he found everything he was looking for in his duties: "A table unsurpassed in delicacies and novelty in terms of the work and dignity, by any French or English lord's table... I always served my dinner as a *maître d'hôtel* and was always complimented." While Talleyrand knew how to revive the *ancien régime's* ostentatiousness because he was not counting pennies, Cambacérès is the spitting image of these "fat republican Midas," mentioned by Grimod and whose pettiness Carême criticized: "All our great culinary talents are languishing due to the miserable thriftiness of rich men, little anxious to earn the fine title of amphitryon" (*L'Art de la Cuisine Française*, p. 8). While Carême was the last *ancien régime*-style *officier de bouche*, he also had experience with the new society and understood the anachronistic nature of his dream: "Here and there, I have strong memories of the great unpleasantnesses caused by the wicked rich; but I must, on the other hand, remember the good ones, the excellent conduct of the gentlemen and true lords I served. I never had reason to complain except with a parvenu, to use the expression with which he ceaselessly referred to himself... The Restoration was not always grand and gracious; I learned a thing or two as M. Le duc de Berry's head chef" ("Une page des *Mémoires,*" art. cit., pp. 215-223).

Since the function of the *maître d'hôtel* in the ancien régime belonged to a past era, Carême considered himself above all an artistic cuisinier, or chef, in search of a patron. This appeal to the rich was better suited to the new society. The rich man should understand "the great importance of having a culinary artist at the head of his household, in order to make the reputation of his table based on the sumptuous fare of the service as a whole; it is the only way to acquire grandeur and dignity in the eyes of the men of power" (*L'Art de la Cuisine Française*, p. 9). The talented chef needs great means to exercise his art. He must be able to improvise by wasting and using a veritable army of servants to execute his culinary plans. This is why Carême left Lord Steward, a gastronomer of renown: "The conditions suited me; but since I was not granted a sufficient staff, I thanked them and withdrew" (*Mémoires*, art. cit.). The art also requires ostentation and brilliant society. At the court of Georges V, Carême felt "discouraged and bored." The lackluster atmosphere lacked magnificence and the artist had no occasion to shine. Carême had a creator's temperament. The greatest joy in his life was when the Emperor Alexander accepted the dedication of his *Projets d'Architecture pour Saint-Pétersbourg:* "A magnificent ring covered with diamonds came with the letter. I received it with tears in my eyes. How wonderful my life had become! My ring was the object of universal curiosity among my colleagues. It was the envy of those who spent their lives in dissipation." Carême insisted on his own talent and personal merits. Through his books he was useful to his colleagues, but he remained jealously protective of his inventions and kept the secret of a certain powder essential in the art of sugar to himself. Like a true artist, he worked alone and relied solely on his own genius. In this regard he is the first artist chef of bourgeois culture, whose attributes were not the sword and court dress but white knee-breeches and a fluted hat.[9]

It is not his serious writing or his pretentious style that earned Carême the title of "the god Carême," but rather his taste for decoration. He was inventive in this domain, and gave free reign to his architectural whims, which could only be executed in exceptional cases: at the celebrations of certain rich individuals and at official ceremonies. In this way he revived the old ornamental tradition of table decoration. Decoration returned with the *beau maigre*, or meatless cooking. In the preface to the *Cuisinier Parisien*, Carême writes that "the experts know how good meatless cooking was once prepared, and how to prepare it today." In reviving meatless cooking, he almost returns to the treatises of the seventeenth and eighteenth centuries. In the eighteenth century, the cooking manual was not based solely on religious prescriptions: it became a dictionary of eating, without reference to holidays and the year according to the church. The return of the *gras* and the *maigre* (the distinction between cooking with and without meat) marks a veritable renaissance in the art of cooking. The Revolution had suppressed Epiphany, the feast of the Kings and *le carême*, or Lent, and conceived of food according to a new and popular culture of drinking songs and banquets. The gastronomical tradition needed meatless cooking to be truly reborn, since it provided the occasion for ornamental research. This is indeed the old domain of the *falsifié,* dishes made to look like things other than what they were, baroque effects and *farces.* For Lent, the chefs created with decorative prowess. In chapter IV of *L'Art Culinaire,* Cussy cites the unpublished *Mémoires of Carême* on this point: "It is in the Lenten cooking that the skill of the chef can make a great impression; this specialty was not swallowed up by our revolutions, which were unbelieving when it came to religious practices. It was at the Elysée Imperial, and through the examples of the famous Laguipierre and Robert, that I was initiated into the work of this fine discipline, which is an ineffable joy. Somehow during the terrible and devastating course of '93 and '94, these strong willed men were respected. When everything had disappeared: the nobility, the clergy, the elegance of the capital, the lively and robust gourmandise of the provinces and even our young and fierce democracy, the specialty of meatless cooking, had been revived, like all that was necessary, under the hand of the valiant first consul. When he came upon the scene, our miseries, as well as those of gastronomy, came to an end. He sent for skilled experts of the *ancien régime,* and prescribed the cuisine of the priesthood and the monarchy for the stomachs of his officers and civil servants. It was necessary, in every respect, to reproduce the great works and thereby to revive them. He gave the orders, and we marched like soldiers. We capitulated as did the whole of Europe! When the Empire came, one heard talk of lean soups and entrées: each year people seized upon the abstinence of Lent as an occasion for culinary feasts full of brilliance and charm. The *beau maigre* first appeared at the home of Mme la Princesse Caroline Murat. Hers was a sanctuary of good living, and Murat was one of the first to do penance, and what a penance!" Thus the Empire revived the *beau maigre.* Curiously the tradition did not fail to make a metaphor of Carême's name in this regard. Lady Morgan cites an astonishing imaginary geneology: "I was already familiar with Carême's treatises, and I was charmed, I must admit, to appreciate them up close. I knew a few characteristics of his family, his origins, his travels. I knew that he was the descendant, through a direct but curious line, of a famous Vatican chef, who, under Léo X, is said to have invented a delicious *maigre* soup to soften the abstinence of the sad *carême,* or Lent: this invention earned him the name Jean de Carême" (cited by Justin Améro, op. cit., p. 279). A. Dumas remarked more simply, "Here is a name that was certainly not destined to acquire the gastronomical celebrity it has achieved." With the *maigre,* the dinner table regained its former splendor. It was within the restricted framework of the small society dinner that Carême first applied the full fire of his passion.

In his *Aphorismes,* Carême speaks of the *petits soupers* of the eighteenth century that brought together "lords and poets," while the nineteenth century dinners assembled "the diplomat, the orator, the member of parliament, the man of letters, the scholar, the artist." The culinary literati created a certain myth of the eighteenth century under the Empire, which would remain in place until the time of the Goncourts. Colnet, Bechoux and the marquis de Cussy made the eighteenth century into an absolute reference point for the art of living and sociality: "The exquisite cuisine born under the illustrious Regent, which next passed to the Condés and the Soubises, often lent a piquant vivacity to the words of Montesquieu, Voltaire, Diderot, Helvétius, d'Alembert, Duclos, Vauvenargues et al., in Paris. But the geniuses paid for these dinners with immortality. How delightful those evenings were then, always too short even though prolonged far into the night. What a sweet and lovable civilization! And what beautiful verses, prospects and ideas it sowed! Yes, it was certainly in the eighteenth century that French society eclipsed all other civilized societies!" The eighteenth-century *petit repas,* organized by a select society, was an event which a certain press *(Le Mercure,* Bachaumont, Grimm*)*, noted just as they would an opera or a play. At the beginning of the nineteenth century, a cultivated and artistic society would amuse itself at meals that were then talked about, and the accounts of which were later saved. Carême, according to Cussy, makes Latin meals, Mme Dacier makes her own broth for her guests her own way, and Mme Vigée-Lebrun makes a Greek supper; on the occasion of this "comedy," she uses accessories from her studio for the decoration and costumes, and

takes the recipes for the sauces from the abbé Barthélémy.[10]

At the baron de Rothschild's house, Carême organized a dinner which, according to Lady Morgan, was "a successful specimen of the current art... entirely in the spirit of the age": "The next day, a fine day in July, at around five o'clock, we set out for the château de Boulogne. It was arranged with much style and splendor. Everything displayed the affection its inhabitants felt for it. We admired the sprigs of beautiful flowers that decorated the entrance. The plants, fruits from every climate scattered here and there, English greenery and French sun, fountains and tropical birds... The party was numerous and brilliant. There were several illustrious foreigners, and the conversation was animated. My eyes rested on a few Flemish tables of remarkable perfection and some beautiful children's toys scattered on the tables in the salon... In spite of the presence of Gérard and Rossini I had only one thought, to judge the clever chef. You can imagine how charmed I was to hear the words, "Madame is served." Everyone rose; we went into the dining room; not like in London, following the orders of the red book, but according to the simple laws of politeness that reserved the best places for the foreigners. The atmosphere was stifling; in spite of the Venetian blinds and awnings, the heat of the drawing rooms was unbearable. It was impossible to serve dinner in the château. The dining room had been transported into the middle of the orange grove, inside a pretty, oblong pavilion of white marble, where the air was freshened by the small fountains nearby, which shot forth pure, sparkling water. The table, set with a cold collation, was covered in the center with an admirably elegant dessert. The day was still clear with the rays of the setting sun, making the silverware sparkle all the more; the china, more precious than gold and silver, due to the perfection of its workmanship, was covered with family scenes. Every detail of the setting reflected a knowledge of life's refinement and an exquisite simplicity. The entrées were placed in a ring around the handsome dessert. The arrangement and the dinner all spoke of Carême: his brilliant variety, his perfect proportions. No more English spices, no more black gravy; on the contrary there were delicate flavors and the taste of truffles... The vegetables retained their natural colors, the mayonnaise seemed to have been fricasseed in snow, like Mme de Sévigné's heart; the ice-cream, with its coolness and the taste of its fruit, replaced the bland English soufflé" (In *La France en 1829 et 1830,* reprinted by Justin Améro, op. cit.). On the dessert, Carême wrote Lady Morgan's name in candied sugar on "a column of the most ingenious architecture." In 1833, he dedicated *l'Art de la Cuisine*

Française to her, specifying that the dinner in Boulogne took place on July 6, 1829.

To the routine of "fine dinners in one of several households and for a limited number of connoisseurs," Carême prefers what he calls the gala events, *les extra, les beaux extra* and *les grands extraordinaires,* since "one must pursue grand operations to become famous." He was at the time an itinerant chef in the service of the art he was helping to evolve. The Empire, with its megalomanic and heroic space, better suited his taste than "the pettiness of the two revolutions that came after 1815." It was at this time that he worked the most under Laguipierre, Robert and Lasne: "My eyes, my poor disenchanted eyes, in this bleak epoch I've come to (May 3, 1830), see no more of the immortal men I once saw, with Caesar at their head, at the dinners and great balls in Paris, Saint-Cloud, Trianon, Compiègne, Fontainebleau and Neuilly; at these brilliant feasts where one was surrounded only by orators and famous generals, and those graceful women in the train of our good and beautiful empress Josephine, who was grace personified, the angel who put our last civil agitations to sleep beneath the tomb" (*Mémoires inédits,* cited in *L'Art Culinaire,* chap. V).

The *grands extra* of the Empire were the great balls of 1810 and 1811, which Carême describes in detail in *Le Pâtissier National.* The festivities of the Empire marked the creation of a new society and the successes of Napoleon: the treatise of Campo-Formio, the return from Egypt, the consulate and the coronation. Carême wrote a "critical review of the three great balls." He tells of "the paltriness of a country wedding." For these grand occasions, one needed an architect's eye, to know how to place and elegantly construct large buffets, "making them easy to approach by the gathered guests." Only the great ceremonies required the skillful calculation of space. In *Le Maître d'hôtel Français,* Carême gives instructions for "a ball for six to a twelve hundred people and even two to three thousand." The buffet system is used for "a high tea or an evening of dancing for 300 guests." "The dancing and the games should not be interrupted by the setting of tables; a single table should be set with 62 articles described in the menu, so that the guests can admire the sight of this elegant type of buffet" (*Le Pâtisseur National,* vol. 2, p. 33). For Louis XVIII's return to Paris, Carême and Lasne, on February 5, 1815, served a meal offered by the royal guard to the national guard (in the great gallery of the Louvre; 1,200 places were set on 12 tables around an orchestra). On February 21, 1816, he was employed for a great ball at the Odéon. This time the national guard invited the royal guard: "In the foyer of the hall, between the stately columns, I had instructed the woodworkers by tracing the central opening and the positioning of a vast, tiered buffet on the floor. In all the window-recesses of the foyer's casement, between the columns, we placed tables only ten inches wide... I can still see the hall of the Odéon sparkling with beauty! the glow of a thousand candles, the columns in the foreground decorated with gold and silver fabrics and an immense crown of flowers bearing the inscription: 'What happy times! We have Louis!.'" "Unfortunately, there was some 'confusion,' for instead of sticking to the order of the buffet, people went to eat in "small groups" in the loggias. During the same period, Carême organized a great military dinner: "From la place Louis XV to la Barrière de l'Étoile, two rows of tables were covered with 10,000 settings." Carême was born too late. Although he was made for the glorious shows of ostentation of the Empire and the architectural constructions of *les grands extraordinaires,* he was forced to preside over the less exalted festivities of the Restoration. In *Le Grand Dictionnaire de Cuisine,* A. Dumas notes, "Carême was brought up on the Empire; one can judge his pain in seeing it crumble. He had to be forced to execute, in *la plaine des Vertus,* the gigantic royal banquet of 1814."

The concern for decor comes into play both in the cooking and the setting, both of which were worked into shapes. The old ornamental cuisine was founded on a certain sense of the baroque. After the food was served, one went on to surprise *farces* and desserts constructed like fireworks, according to the trompe l'oeil tradition of the *leurre* which, by way of the Middle

Ages, went all the way back to Latin cooking. Carême wanted to replace this sparkling profusion with a new decorative cuisine characterized by "elegance" and a working of pastry that related to drawing and architecture. In *L'Art de la Cuisine Française au XIXeme siècle* (p. 7), he notes the progress in the new type of serving: "In order to follow our gastronomical and culinary dissertations, we invite our colleagues to consider Vincent la Chappelle's drawing of a table opposite my drawing of a table with eighty settings, through which I set up my parallel between old and new cooking... In truth, there was no elegance then. Furthermore, the profusion with which the tables of the rich eighteenth-century hosts were covered, bears witness to the immense progress made by the alimentary arts in the nineteenth century." In *Le Maître d'hôtel,* he criticizes the extreme size of the entrées, the large dishes and especially the lack of distance between "the placement of the guests at table": "Given the diameters of the plates as they had been placed, there were only eighteen inches for the placement of each person." A comparison of the drawings by la Chapelle (1736) and Carême clearly demonstrates the transformation of table settings. The crowding, unselfconsciousness and a certain off-handedness in the profusion itself gave way to a more airy and functional order. Air circulated between the dishes. The former presentation, in the too vertical and anarchic pyramid that produces a fine effect but remains inaccessible, later becomes as dated and "gothic" as yesterday's high coiffures. Carême's table "is nothing like a wig" says Lady Morgan. The taste of the day requires a clearer order in which it finds a new elegance.

Through the critique of *l'ambigu,* the cold collation, Carême defines his concept of the new culinary taste: "I had promised to take charge of the *ambigu,* a bizarre, ridiculous service detrimental to our art. If one isn't careful, good cooking will become impoverished and insipid; for why cook well and serve hot if the dishes are only eaten cold, or at the very best tepid?... Good cooking loses its fresh appearance and its quality when served this way, which decidedly prevents one from savoring the dishes with the ineffable pleasure good living affords. Luckily for us, there are still certain households in which the good hosts... reject the baroque *ambigu;* for what could be more ridiculous that to see a confused amalgamation of entrées and entremets, both of which are eaten indiscriminately by certain guests who make no effort to be fine connoisseurs?" It is in *L'Art de bien traiter* of 1693, that the first definition of *l'ambigu* appeared: "This method is very stylish and popular both because one can easily reconcile and mix many different types of things together...

This way of serving is, properly speaking, a combined supper and collation and is usually given at the end of the day; instead of dividing a meal into several courses, everything is put together beforehand, with an orderly and well defined execution. The idea is good, but it is difficult to execute well, and it is no small feat to arrange a banquet of this nature." This method of serving thus offers hashes and jams at the same time. It had pleasing elements for Carême, given its decorative nature. He rarely used it, however, except in unusual cases such as the Boulogne dinner in the late afternoon, in the middle of orange groves, or at the *grands extra* with buffets. This was because the *ambigu* produced a suspicious and disorderly effect, a sort of gustative cacophony. Carême's culinary innovations show the same distaste for mixtures and hybrid productions: "What could be more ridiculous and absurd than to see people serve, for example, alongside pike and carp *à la Chambord,* garnishings made of sweetbreads laced with lard, innocent pigeons, cockscombs and cock's kidneys? Such was nonetheless the custom of the most well-reputed men of the time. Upon further reflection, one might well say that the genius of these great practitioners had not yet understood the ridiculousness of serving butcher's meats with fowl and fish; whereas it was so easy to change this ancient custom through the infinite variety offered by working in fish fillets such as sole, trout, mackerel, salmon and others, and by serving them in steaks, in *attereaux Conty* with truffles, in *quenelles* with truffles or mushrooms, or with *ravigote* sauce. It was at the house of the Regent of Great Britain that, for the first time, I served my pike *à la regence,* surrounded by rich garnishings made up of all types of fish" (*L'Art de la Cuisine Française,* p. 7). This culinary reform bans the marriage of opposites. In decoration, one was not to "mask the dishes" with "ingredients" that had no relationship to them. Antiquated, pernicious medleys of pots-pourris and hotchpotches are just "hodgepodges." Carême seeks a cuisine of distinct tones, in which the flavors are on the same register, a culinary monochrome. In the name of taste, and in deference to the eyes, the art must play on measured spaces and sweet harmonies.

Between the food and the gold and silver plates that hold them, there must be a subtle decorative harmony. For the new cuisine, Carême prefers round and oval shapes to the "square, octagonal and festooned" dishes. Inversely, he conceived of "skewers" for serving the large meats, in order to bring them to the same level of elegance as the gilded bronzes, crystals, "fine works of goldsmithing by Odiot, Bienet, August and Lebrun." In *Le Cuisinier Parisien* (preface, p. 23), Carême explains his collaboration with

Odiot: "I was quite fortunate to have M. Odiot execute drawings in goldwork in the style of my new goblets; consequently, the second serving corresponds perfectly to the elegance and the richness of the first. Likewise the silverware of M. le baron de Rothschild is without a doubt one of the most beautiful and elegant in all Paris. It does honor to the craftsmanship of M. Odiot." The two men had many things in common. Odiot also owed his success to the Empire. He had worked for Napoleon and Josephine and fashioned two famous objects, the dressing table for Marie-Louise, and the cradle-rocker for the king of Rome. Like Carême, he was passionate about drawing. The goldsmith and the chef used a similar repertory of forms borrowed from architecture and sculpture. In food, only sugar could be worked like bronze. Thus Carême made pastry-making his specialty, to satisfy his decorative penchant. In *Le Pâtissier Pittoresque* he shows drawings to which he "devoted all the free time" of his life. Since the Middle Ages, with the tinkling fountains and oriental mechanics, dessert has been the domain of magic and spectacle. For Carême, it was the occasion for an astonishing search for ornamental effects.

In the seventeenth century, decoration allowed the host to inscribe his personal qualities into the food, to stamp it with a social signature. The insignia of the household did not appear only in the goldwork, table settings and centerpieces, but in the food itself. One "arranged" historic salads and gave them "garnishings and ornament." Pierre de Lune, in *Le Parfait Confiturier* of 1669, indicates many types of crowns for *salades couronnés:* "royal, princely, ducal, of a marquis, a count," etc. Following the same principle, Carême tailored the decoration to the meal itself. Ornamental motifs displayed the signs and symbols of the gathered society at the table: "One should, it seems to me, match the decorations to the gatherings at the tables we are serving. For example, for a military meal, helmets and trophies; for musicians, the lyre and the harp; for a marriage, the temple of hymen; for philosophers, pavilions and cottages; for novelists, ruins, waterfalls, fountains, towers, forts, rocks and torrents; something to satisfy everyone" (*Le Pâtisseur Parisien,* p. 412). Food is never naked, but surrounded by accessories and presented on a base. Carême was the first to use lard in this construction of bases in low relief. One still finds vestiges of this today in butchers' windows in France, in the lard and sugar ballerinas and swans. In this light, Carême appears as a frustrated architect.

Les Projets d'architecture for the beautifying of Paris and Saint-

Petersburg are presented as the fruit of leisure time and a consolation in suffering. Carême was "struck with admiration for the great monuments of Egypt, Greece and Italy," and could not resist "the enthusiasm aroused by the appearance of the truly beautiful." For la place du Carrousel, he planned a great temple devoted to the glories of the French nation, with "48 lions heads, 12 trophies, 8 statues, the names of the kings and the great men who added to the lustre of France." For desserts, architectural constructions were the fashion.[11] Carême went about them with a particular seriousness and a taste for the monumental. In *Le Pâtissier National* he describes a grandiose consecrated bread: "This large composition produces an admirable effect; it was executed in Neuilly for the duchess, who was to present it as an homage to the parish church. When I had finished this consecrated bread, and it was in the middle of the church, I found that it had a grand, religious quality, surrounded by the incense that was burning in the small incense-burners and cups and soon perfumed the sacred vault of the temple" (4th part, p. 74). While for set pieces Grimod preferred frivolous subjects such as the representation of operatic scenes, Carême tended toward a more restrained culture. In the dessert, he placed the virtuous and gloomy gallery of the bourgeois pantheon: "The *entremets* I recommended to them (the pastry chefs of the house) is a large fountain of Parnassus. I executed it twice to serve at my grand dinners; it produced the same effect I anticipated. This dish is mounted in the shape of an ancient fountain, crowned with a palm wreath and two laurel wreaths decorating the two sides of the piece. In these crowns I placed the names of Sophocles, Schiller, Shakespeare and Racine... I made these large centerpieces yet again for another grand dinner, and in the four crowns I put the names of four great poets: Homer, Virgil, Dante, Milton. To make these centerpieces more nationalistic when they are served at a minister's table, one could put the names of the abbé Suger, l'Hôpital, Sully and Colbert in the crowns. For a field-marshal's table, one could use the names of Condé, Bayard, Vendôme and Turenne. For an admiral, one might put the names of Dugay-Trouin, Tourville, Jean Bart and Suffren in the crowns. For the dinners of scholars and artists, one could adjust the laurel crowns decorating the two sides of the centerpiece, then use inscriptions to recall the illustrious names of our poets, painters, sculptors and artists in every field." Carême had the curious desire to create durable objects in the fragile stuff of pastry-making. He succeeded in preserving a military trophy for six years, due to a special mastic of an antique bronze color. The project of a small monument composed "for the return of the king" in 1815 and never executed, lies somewhere between architecture and pastry-making. "Anxious to execute several large center-pieces that could be preserved for a good number of years without the slightest alteration," Carême decided to replace the decorative sugar work that "falls apart in humid weather," with a more resilient material made out of gum arabic, gum dragon, sugar, starch, and marble dust.

Carême, called by Cussy "the Palladio of the kitchen," had made an in-depth study of drawing, at the print collection of the royal library. *Le Pâtissier Pittoresque* includes a "treatise of the five orders of architecture according to Vignola," and "details from the Caryatidal, Paestum, Egyptian, Chinese and Gothic orders, drawn from the *Parallèle des Monuments antiques et modernes.*" The drawings shown are models for large centerpieces, whose dimensions are cited by Carême in *Le Pâtissier Parisien:* "These large centerpieces have a diameter of from 48 to 65 centimeters, and their height ranges from one to one and a half meters." The subjects include decorative motifs that mix different times and cultures, in an encyclopedic fashion: pavilions, rotundas, temples, ruins, towers, gazebos, forts, waterfalls, fountains, summer houses, thatched cottages, windmills and hermitages, which are Italian, Turkish, Muslim, Russian, Polish, Venetian, Chinese, Irish, Gallic and Egyptian in style. For the table settings, one had to ensure the harmonies and contrasts in the centerpieces' combinations: "A vase should be set with an elegant basket, a light cup with a cassolette, just as a lyre should be served with a harp, an ancient helmet with a modern one, a war trophy with a naval trophy; likewise a thatched hut with a rustic grotto, a Chinese pavilion with a Turkish pavilion, a temple with a rotunda, a pediment with a column, an Egyptian fountain with a modern fountain, a waterfall with a waterfall. Furthermore, an ancient ruin should be set with a modern one, a gazebo with a fort, and so on, as one can see in the drawings (*Le Pâtissier Parisien,* 3rd part, p. 412). Carême derives his astonishing drawings from his travel experiences and autodidactic readings. He seems to have been inspired primarily by the art of gardens.[12] Aside from such theoreticians of picturesque gardens as Watelet, Duchesne, Giradin and Morel, Carême could have consulted *Les Maisons de Campagne* by Kraft (1750), and especially the series by Le Rouge (*Jardins anglo-chinois* or *Détail des nouveaux jardins à la mode*) published from 1774 to 1789. His models for centerpieces are, in principle, quite close to the structures for gardens, those small, isolated and free-standing constructions which, for this reason, can be used in all possible combinations. The seventeenth-century garden structures display the same prototypes as Carême's models: kiosks, pagodas, Chinese pavilions (Chanteloup, Betz), minarets, Turkish and Tartar tents (Monceau, Menars), temples (Petit Trianon, Ermenonville, Méréville), gazebos (Versailles). The system of structures and models used as elements in a game of construction corresponds to that late eighteenth-century learning which created the forms of a collective imaginary world. The tabular configuration of the models and structures can only be understood in terms of the vogue for dictionaries, illustrated texts, encyclopedic classification and Condillac's associative analysis of the progress of human knowledge. This is why Carême worked so hard at putting all human culture into his cakes. In the combination of motifs and styles, he goes so far as to syncretize the most fantastic and outrageous elements: his Gallic hermitage is a sort of Byzantine cottage; in the "great Roman ruin," a surprising clock reads eight o'clock. The model for the most unusual set piece is without a doubt the "military prison." The artist chef was undoubtedly fascinated by the monumental character of this subject. All the same, with this project he conceived the most phantasmagorical cake of the nineteenth century.

The technique of spun sugar allowed one to imitate "the waves of the ocean," the sails of a ship, and to execute the most difficult subjects: "waterfalls, rivers, palm trees, sparks, straw for thatched roofs, the wings of windmills, the sails of small gondolas, temples, ruins, balls, heavenly and celestial orbs, strings with which to decorate elegant harps and lyres, and especially to make the plumes and tails of antique and modern helmets" (*Le Pâtissier Parisien*, 3rd part, p. 348). In his *sultane en surprise*, Carême works the sugar like a glassmaker. He makes a globe of threaded sugar and inside places a "beautiful bouquet of pretty spring flowers."

Some chefs do not like "decor" because they are incapable of satisfying the senses of both taste and sight: "No doubt vulgar men feel contempt for the most beautiful ornament of our art: why? Because they can produce nothing that could be both attractive to the eye and sensually pleasing. Their bad taste inspires only poor and narrow-minded ideas; in the sad compositions of their decorations, they use only things that are in reality inedible" (preface to *Le Pâtissier Parisien*). With Carême, everything is edible, and this produces distortions and surprising divergences in the visual and gustative effects. The rocks must be edible. The "moss covered grotto" is made of hard sweetmeats: "The effect of this large centerpiece is very picturesque. It is round in shape and has four arcades. It is made of hard sweetmeat *à la reine,* which must also be glazed: one part with rose-colored sugar, one with caramelized sugar, and the rest with lump sugar to which you add saffron: but in removing the hard sweetmeats from the saucepan, you form groups from five to eight and from ten to twelve, over which you sprinkle coarse sugar and chopped pistachios" (Le Pâtissier Parisien, 4th part, p. 44). The rocks are piles of small cakes: "The rock forms four arcades, which are made up of ring biscuits of almond puff pas-

try (which you powder with fine sugar sifted through silk). You simply line up these ring biscuits without attaching them at the vertical joins, which in no time produces a nice ridge of rocks. You surround it with meringues glazed and garnished with vanilla cream. The pedestal is made of German waffles; the garnish is Genoese pastries in rings, studded with sugar pearls. The bower is crowned with a small waterfall in silvery spun sugar" (Le Pâtissier Parisien, 4th part, p. 43). In the "Ruin of Palmyra," in order to "trace the ruin's outlines," one should use thick pastry dough with "yellow sugar mixed with red and green, which makes a granite color." This is how one eats dazzling things, ruins and mosses. It is particularly in the rocks that pastry-making and the art of gardens come together. In the seventeenth century, Pierre de Lune, in *Le Parfait Confiturier*[13] (1668), explains how to group "orange slices into rocks," and to "whip cream" with small elm branches to "stiffen" it to make "whipped-cream rocks." Inversely, from the time of the seventeenth century, the rocks and grottoes, which would become the principal accessory of gardens, looked like pastry because they were agglomerations of strange materials covered with shells and bits of rock crystal. Some rocks are made out of cloth or cardboard, or are painted wood like stage scenery.[14] The same deceptive effect is at work in the Ermenonville "dessert" and Carême's ruins. But with Carême the trompe-l'oeil effect brings into play the whole gamut of flavors.

In his *Revue Critique des grand bals de 1810-1811,* Carême begins by criticizing the colors of foods: "This is what I see: aspics that are too strongly colored, which makes the sad decoration invisible; fowl in galantine glazed with a black glaze; suspicious-looking sauces with strange hues. The fish entrées are arranged in a dreadful fashion... Then to brighten up these sad entrées, they are edged with badly cut jelly, placed haphazardly; and to give more spark to this jelly, many different colors have been mixed in" (*Le Pâtissier Parisien,* p. 421). The artist chef must be a tasteful colorist. The light and soft tints, like that of "red sugar," are the only truly elegant ones: "We give these colored sugars only the lightest of tints: for the more delicate the color, the prettier and more pleasing to the eye" (*Le Pâtissier Parisien,* p. 77). For "the Bower with trellis decorated with grapes," the trellis is made of "pale green pastry dough" and the wood "chocolate colored." For "The Gothic Cup with a basket decorated with laurel leaves," one uses "white and lilac almond paste." Lady Morgan specifies that in the "composition" of the Boulogne meal, there were no "strongly spiced sauces, black gravies, tastes of Cayenne pepper or of allspice, caramel, *pain brûlé*": "Each dish had its natural flavor; all the vegetables retained their green hue" (*La France en 1829-1830,* p. 323). It is through the clear unctuousness of the new tints that Carême breaks the most definitively with the old cuisine. His chef's palette banishes all the dark tones in favor of blond sauces. His culinary creations do not have a dark background like Dutch painting, but rather the intense freshness of Gérard's glazes, the acid and lemony tints of Caspar David Friedrich. Food, for Carême, is given back its own essences and contains, already, the virginal seeds of Manet's and Proust's asparagus. It is in his taste for light colors that Carême was in perfect agreement with "the delicate luxury and exquisite sensuality of the Empire." A meal by Carême should be imagined in the context of the beautiful Compiègne Empire-style dining room, whose soft orange hue contrasts subtly with the black sconces.

Carême does not concern himself with the literary effects that Grimod de La Reynière calls "gourmand writing." Through his simplifying work in cooking and serving, he founds the national bourgeois cuisine of the nineteenth century. This traveling chef who roamed Europe and lived through revolutions, experienced the profound change in social structures through the ritual of the meal as a private gathering or collective celebration. As a pastry chef, he uses the elements of a syncretic imaginary realm in his decor, relying on the architecture, the art of gardens and the culture of his age. Certainly with Carême we are not presented with the daily life or the sensibility of an epoch. He does, however, give us a sense of just how rigid and restrictive is the sort of literary history that chooses not to consider the "sense" that is at times at stake in a simple cake.

Previously published in *Romantisme: Revue du dix-neuvième siècle*, No. 17-8, 1977.

Translated by Sophie Hawkes

Notes

1. *officier de bouche; homme de bouche:* Under the ancien régime, a group of officers attached to serving the royal table; the *service de bouche* included 7 *offices* and more than 500 *officiers*.
2. "Delille of the dinner table": a reference to the poet l'Abbé Jacques Delille, known as a skillful versifier.
3. *Le Caveau moderne:* Bacchic and poetic society founded by Crébillon père (Le Caveau), disbanded in 1739 and reformed twenty years later by Crébillon fils under the name of *Le Caveau moderne*.
4. Bibliography of Carême (1784-1833):
Le Pâtissier royal parisien: an elementary and practical treatise on old and new pastry-making, desserts, cold entrées and bases, followed by useful observations on the progress of this art, a series of more than sixty menus, and a critical review of the great balls of 1810 and 1811. Written by M. A. Carême, in Paris, the pastry chef of grands extraordinaires. This work is illustrated with over seventy plates drawn by the author. 1815, 2 vols. in-8.
Le Maître d'Hôtel Français traces a parallel between old and new cooking, considered from the point of view of the arrangement of menus, according to the four seasons. This work contains an account of the menus served in Paris, Saint-Petersburg, London and Vienna. By A. Carême of Paris. 1822, 2 vols. in-8.
Le Cuisinier Parisien, elementary and practical treatise on cold entrées, pedestals and sweet dishes, followed by useful observations on the progress of these two aspects of modern cooking. Illustrated with twenty-five plates drawn by the author. 1828, in-8.
Projets d'architecture, intended to embellish Paris and Saint-

Petersburg, drawn from sketches by the author... (2 collections in-folio made up of 6 installments which appeared between 1821 and 1826).

L'Art de la Cuisine Française of the nineteenth century. Elementary and practical treatise on clear meat and meatless stocks, extracts, high-flavored concentrates, French and foreign soups, fish main courses; complex and simple sauces, ragouts and garnishes; main courses of beef, ham, fowl and game, followed by culinary and gastronomical discussions useful to the progress of this art. 1833-1835, 3 vols. in-8.

Le Pâtissier Pittoresque, written and illustrated by Antonin Carême, from Paris, containing one hundred and twenty-five engraved plates of which one hundred and ten depict a variety of models, pavilions, rotundas, temples, ruins, towers, gazebos, forts, waterfalls, fountains, summer houses, thatched cottages, windmills and hermitages, preceded by a treatise on the five orders of architecture according to Vignola, to which details on the Caryatid, Paestum, Egyptian, Chinese and Gothic orders have been added, drawn from the *Parallèle des Monuments antiques et modernes.* New, revised and much expanded edition in 1854, in-8 (First edition, 1815).

5. In the entry on Carême in the *Grand Dictionnaire de Cuisine,* A. Dumas tells in melodramatic style of the difficult beginnings of the worthy chef: "Like all founders of empires, such as Theseus or Romulus, Carême is a sort of lost child. He was born in Paris on June 7, 1784, in a construction site on the rue de Bac where his father worked. With fifteen children and no idea how to feed them all, one evening his father took little Marie-Antoine, aged eleven, to dine at the town gates. Then, leaving him in the middle of the sidewalk, he said to him, 'Run along, little one, there are fine trades in this world; leave us to languish, misery is our fate, we shall die in it...'"

6. *nef, cadenas:* pieces of goldsmithing in the shape of a boat and a chest, respectively, used to hold a lord's table setting and presented to him at the beginning of a meal.

7. See the texts cited by A. Franklin in volume eight of *L'Histoire de la Vie Privée des Français* (p. 190-196).

8. See Pierre David's definition of the duties of the maître d'hôtel in his *Maître d'hostel* of 1639: "The hour of the meal having come, he takes a white towel, which he folds lengthwise and places on his shoulder as usual, as this is the mark of his power and the particular and demonstrative symbol of his Duty. He can serve with a sword at his side, a coat on his back and a hat on his head, but always... It is noteworthy that during the meal he has the power to command all the household servants... His duty is to make provisions for those in his care."

In chapter VII of *l'Art Culinaire,* Cussy explains Carême's vocation of maître d'hôtel: "Carême supplemented his special talents as a chef with those of coordinator, director and the very difficult talent of Maître d'hôtel. The chef with great ideas always has something of the administrator in him: but he has to be this man. When Carême studied his profession, when he learned its secrets, he deduced from them a complete theory of serving, drawn from his experience and the things he had read. He composed the dishes and courses of menus according to the seasons, and specified the costs of purchases, rules of conservation, duties of the officers and the aides; he created his own *Maître d'hôtel*."

9. In *Le Maître d'hôtel Français* (p. 278), Carême explains how he wore a rigid chef's hat for the first time. In one illustration he compares the old chef in his floppy hat that looks like a nightcap, with the new, noble bearing of the artist chef: "Ceaselessly meditating on the elegance of our work, for a long time I pondered a means of wearing our cotton caps in a different way; it seemed essential to me not to change this cap, whose whiteness compliments the rest of our outfit... When I had the idea of wearing my cap garnished with a round piece of cardboard (one could also make it octagonal), it became more graceful; I was in Vienna on my first voyage in 1821. Each day around eleven o'clock in the morning, I presented his Excellency Lord Steward the dinner menu. The ambassador looked at me, smiled, and said to me, 'This new headdress is better suited to a chef.' I noted to his Excellency that a chef should look like a man in good health, whereas our ordinary cap is more reminiscent of the state of convalescence."

10. This is how Mme Vigée-Lebrun recounts her famous Greek supper (cited in *l'Histoire de l'alimentation* by D. A. Gottschalk): "Since my supper has become historic, and since it has become a Roman orgy, I shall describe it to you in all its simplicity. One evening when I had invited twelve to fifteen people to dinner, my brother had read a few pages of the *Voyages d'Anacharsis* beforehand... Since we were expecting some very pretty women, I imagined us all dressed as Greeks, in order to surprise M. de Vaudreuil. My studio, which was full of everything I needed to drape my models, furnished me with enough clothing, and the Comte de Parois, who lodged in my house, had a superb collection of Etruscan vases. He brought me a large number of cups and vases, which I placed on a mahogany table without a tablecloth. This done, behind the chairs I placed an immense screen, which I hid by covering it with a white curtain, attached at intervals such as one sees in the paintings of Poussin. A suspended lamp cast a strong light on the table... "

11. In song IV of *La Gastronomie,* entitled "Dessert," Berchoux describes the centerpieces:

> To the aid of the dessert call in all the arts,
> Especially the one that shines in the Lombard quarter.
> There, you're certain to find, to your heart's content,
> Sweets arranged into gay buildings,
> Castles made of bonbons, biscuit palaces,
> The Louvre, Bagatelle and Versailles preserved;
> The loves of Sappho, Abelard and Tibullus,
> Camacho's wedding and the labors of Hercules,

And a thousand other things that are imitated
By clever sweetmeat makers I could mention by name.
Don't destroy these sugary marvels,
Prepared to charm your eyes alone:
Or at least wait a few days, in order to grant
These sweet monuments a few days' respite.

12. I heartily thank Monique Mosser who, at the time in which she was preparing the exhibition "Gardens of France (1760-1820)," shown at the Hôtel de Sully from May 18 to September 11, 1977, showed me a series of structures which might have inspired Carême. For further information on these structures, see Monique Mosser, "M. de Marigny et les jardins (projets inédits des fabriques pour Menars)" *Bulletin de la Société de l'Histoire de l'Art français,* 1972; Ernest de Ganay, "Fabriques aux jardins du XVIIIème siècle (Edifice de la Chine et de l'Orient, temples, pavilions, belvédères)," *Revue de l'Art ancien et modern,* vol. LXIV, June-December 1933.

13. Pierre de Lune writes, "In a large bowl, place a half-litre mug of soft cream, take a fistful of elm branches well peeled and cleaned; whip the cream well and add some powdered sugar and gum dragon until it becomes as thick as butter, arrange it in pieces on a plate; it rises as high as one likes and will remain in this state for two days if sugar is not put on top of it."

14. See Ernest de Ganay, "Les Rochers et les Eaux dans les Jardins à l'Anglaise," *Revue de l'Art ancien et moderne,* no. cit., pp. 63-80.

Cyber Space Foods
VRcades Project 9602

Jon McKenzie

VRcades, a research group located in New York at the intersection of Electronic Media and Cultural Theory, is pleased to announce the formation of an alliance with Caroline La Motte, Doctor of Interfacial Performance.

The alliance between Dr. La Motte and VRcades is called Cyber Space Foods. The mission of Cyber Space Foods is to develop human-computer interfaces which utilize the chemical senses of taste and smell. By bringing together our research on oral and nasal technologies, the alliance seeks to invent new modes of interfacial performance.

A few words about our qualifications: Dr. La Motte has specializations in audiovisual and digestive tracking systems. She is also a master chef, and this training informs all of her research: "Interface design has thus far been dominated by the eyes, ears, and hands of engineers. My work begins with the orifice of eating." The doctor approached VRcades after learning of our own work on *The Bureau of Traces,* a machine for inventing theoretical perfumes.

Based on our mutual interests, Cyber Space Foods was formed the last week of December, 1995, at a breakfast meeting in Chicago. The charter of the alliance details its technical and theoretical directives:

In researching taste and smell, we do not seek to replace what Hegel called the theoretical senses of hearing and seeing. Nor will we simply drop or abandon touch. Cyber Space Foods acknowledges the important role played on the computer by the eyes, ears, and hands. But the alliance seeks to reengineer these senses within the new sensorium of cyberspace, a space constituted less by forms and developments than by currents and break-downs. Because smell and taste perceive flows and par-ticles of matter, Cyber Space Foods believes they will become the guiding senses of electronic media. Our mis-sion is therefore quite simple: to put noses and mouths on all our interfaces.

During the preliminary meetings between Dr. La Motte and VReades, we decided that Cyber Space Foods would first focus its research on the interface potential of taste. The following is a report on the opportunities and difficulties facing our work.

Who or What's on the Menu?

One of the most fruitful areas of investigation stems from this insight, first articulated by Dr. La Motte. "It's important to real-ize that the computer is already gastronomic. The interface developed by Apple—and later copied by Microsoft and others—involves selecting items from *menus*. To study these menus, one must approach the desk-top as a table in a restaurant and then start inquir-ing into the relationship between ordering and eat-ing."

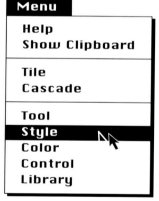

The importance of this insight is twofold: first, because menus are distributed across a wide range of computer platforms, they reveal a strategic site for conceptualizing oral interfaces. Menus can be found in operating systems as well as such applica-tions as word processors, spreadsheets, and com-munications software. Second, Dr. La Motte's insight connects this orality to the command center of human-computer interfaces, for menus are lists of orders, arrangements of the command languages through which people and machines interact. "Ordering" or selecting an item from a menu, a person's performance cues another performance, that of the computer.

These considerations have led Dr. La Motte to another important insight, namely, *menus are rituals of sociotechnic feedback.* As durable goods, computers are consumed in their interaction with human operators. In turn, the labor of these operators is itself consumed through such performances as pointing, clicking, and typing. The ritual of this sociotechnic consumption sets up a circuit of command performances, the *feedback* of humans and computers. Who's eating what? What's ordering whom? These are the questions effacing those who develop oral interfaces.

Cyber Space Foods has begun to elaborate on Dr. La Motte's insights. Primary among our efforts is the compilation of a Megamenu, a giant menu composed of thousands upon thousands of other menus. By collecting and annotating all their orders into one Megamenu, our alliance will generate a gastronomic guide to the feedback of humans and machines.

Recipes for Machinic Orality

A second and closely related area of research which Dr. La Motte brought to the table was first staked out by the French philosopher Félix Guattari, whom she met at a dinner honoring Prof. William Rutherford. At the time of their meeting, Dr. La Motte was already a voracious reader of Guattari, especially of his *Chaosmosis,* wherein the Frenchman examines this order, "Don't speak with your mouth full, it's very bad manners!" Guattari writes:

> You either speak or you eat. Not both at the same time. On one side a differentiated flux—the variety of food taken up in a process of disaggregation, chaotisation, sucked up by an inside of flesh—and on the other side, a flux of elementary articulations—phonological, syntactical, propositional—which invests and constitutes a complex, differentiated outside. But strictly speaking, orality is at the intersection. It speaks with its mouth full. It is full of inside and full of outside.

Looking over her menu, Dr. La Motte expressed a desire to prepare *hors-d'oeuvres* and command languages to feed into this mouth, this strange orifice which Guattari calls *machinic orality.*

Cyber Space Foods understands machinic orality as a challenge to the prohibition against mixing words and things, complexity and chaos. Machinic orality feeds on orders, or what Guattari prefers to call order words. Feeding back on order words, machinic orality fast forwards the linear voice of command languages straight into the teeth of multiheaded desiring-machines.

Aesthetic practices offer excellent channels for such unreserved feasting, especially practices drawn from performance art. Guattari writes that "Such art doesn't so much involve a return to an originary orality as it does a forward flight... into machinic paths capable of engendering mutant subjectivities." Part subject, part object, machinic orality partitions the voice with flows of sounds, gestures, and images, with intricate performances such as banquets and other consumptive rituals which can gather social forces around such simple events as the breaking of bread or the drinking of coffee.

As an *hors-d'oeuvre* to her Megamenu, Dr. La Motte is concocting recipes programmed by the taste buds of machinic orality. She calls them "Machinic Recipes." This is how to speak with a mouthful: First, select and mix order words from different menus. Next, extract from these orders singular affects or microperceptions. These bits of sensation are then digested so as to contaminate not the raw and the cooked, but the cook and the cooked. Guattari describes this last step: "Something is absorbed—incorporated, digested—from which new lines of meaning take shape and are drawn out... The blocks of sensation of machinic orality detach a deterritorialised flesh from the body. When I 'consume' a work... I carry out a complex ontological crystallization..."

from the kitchen of
Caroline La Motte

1. Select order words.
2. Extract and prepare singular affects.
3. Digest and become-other.

The Machinic Recipes developed by Dr. La Motte are designed to produce lines of cybernautic flight, an experience or experiment spiced with human and technological ingredients. Words and bodies, food bites and computer bytes: this is the fourfold unfolding of autopoetic feedback. In short order: the mixing of commands and foods takes off into the becoming-wired of organic humanism.

For Cyber Space Foods, the menu is thus the thing to be eaten. On some occasions, Machinic Recipes are to be served with a specially prepared relish. As Dr. La Motte states, "One must learn to confuse menus and meals in order to develop a taste for order words." She goes on to argue that, "by ingesting these recipes, we'll stop all this silly talk about computer menus being *metaphors*."

Reformatting the Java Drive

A third area of research is most stimu-
lating: it concerns the marketing of
Cyber Space Foods to consumers. Like
computer menus, this area indicates
that oral interfaces are already installed
world wide and across the Web. As Dr. La
Motte is fond of saying, "one only has to wake up and smell
them." This third area of research is the drive connecting com-
puter addicts and coffee fiends.

Throughout 1995, the World Wide Web was abuzz with the
release of Java, a high performance programming language
developed by Sun Microsystems. Java provides programmers a
language for writing across the different platforms and browsers
used on the Web. Small, portable applications called Java applets
can travel rapidly across the Internet to perform a specific event
on a specific machine—and then automatically trash them-
selves.

These nomadic, ephemeral applets are now transforming the
command performances of human-computer interaction. Object
oriented, real time, and jargon compliant, Java portends a muta-
tion of cyberspace: supplementing the absolute space of main-
frame terminals and the localized space of PCs, Java percolates
in the catastrophic space of local absolutes, a space in which
orders and recipes fly quickly between servers and clients.

Cyber Space Foods is using Java to program Machinic Recipes
which will be served in the disastrous space of the Web. At the
same time, however, we are decoding Java in order to analyze
the wiring diagram of its cultural inscription. After consuming
several films on Indonesian drinking rituals, Dr. La Motte is
reheating Java as an allegorical program for becoming-wired, for
the ontological jitters and the multimedia rush which can occur
in interfacial performances.

Stimulated by her consumption of Java, Dr. La Motte has engi-
neered a startling gastronomic discovery: the computer, having
already eaten the typewriter and the telephone, has begun to
ingest coffee machines and certain of their consumptive rituals.
The reason for this is simple: computers crave a blend of effi-
ciency and creativity, and to stimulate them in humans, they are
now daisy-chaining themselves to a socially prescribed caffeine
addiction. Further, by ingesting the rituals of this addiction,
computers have begun to reformat our Java Drive.

Jon McKenzie

The reformatted Java Drive is the target market of Cyber Space Foods. In other words, we target the electronic displacement of caffeinated rituals, specifically those sociotechnic performances which support efficiency and creativity. In the gastrontology of coffee beans, three ritual machines are of special interest to our marketing researchers.

First, the coffee break, which has long been a ritual mixing caffeinated drinks and informal reflection upon the corporate workplace. Yet this consumption of coffee, tea, and soft drinks, as well as the break itself, is institutionally staged to provide workers with caffeine so as to increase their productive efficiency.

A second ritual machine involves hanging out in cafes or expresso bars, traditionally gathering sites for artists and writers who live off the crust and crumbs of the business world. Here caffeine is consumed for the stimulating effects it has upon nonproductive creativity.

Now to nourish its craving for a blend of efficient and creative beings, the computer contributes to the hybridization of workplace and cafe rituals. This process has produced a third ritual machine, that of dining at cybercafes. Cybercafe menus include food and computer activities and attract a mixed clientele composed of hackers and artists, anarchists and technocrats.

Dr. La Motte is currently doing fieldwork in American cybercafes in order to study how the Java Drive is being reformatted. She states that "in the last four decades, the computer has been slowly weaning humans from caffeine to software. Having identified coffee as a stimulant to efficiency and creativity, the computer has started to replace java with Java." Indeed, since the late 1950s, the percentage of Americans who consume coffee has declined by 25%. At the same time, the use of computers has spread from select science and military labs to millions and millions of businesses and homes. According to the doctor, our withdrawal from caffeine has been tempered by a new and growing addiction: America Online.

Cybercafes offer excellent sites to study the reformatting of our Java Drive and to analyze different blends of creativity and efficiency. Cyber Space Foods believes such traits will help us understand how oral interfaces connect to different systems of sociotechnic evaluation. In addition to our research on the Java Drive, we will also use cybercafes to conduct electronic taste tests of Megamenu orders and Machinic Recipes.

188

Cybernausea and the Vomit Comet

Several challenges confront Cyber Space Foods. Among them are the notorious difficulties which can arise when flows of languages and foods, humans and computers, all gather round a table. Many an interface has been ruined by the crumbs of a sticky breakfast roll. Needless to say, before any public electronic taste tests can be performed, Cyber Space Foods must address this and other problems.

As a matter of safety, VReades technicians will work closely with NASA food scientists in order to draw upon their knowledge of hardware-safe nutritional items. Astronauts have been mixing commands and foods for decades. Before any food takes flight, however, it must first be tested by NASA personnel on the KC-135, a zero-gravity airplane affectionately known as the "Vomit Comet." NASA scientists use the Vomit Comet to test foods for how they will react in micro-gravity. A food item is added to the menu only after it has undergone all the necessary research and testing. Only those foods which stay down can take flight.

Of course, Cyber Space Foods is less interested in space flights than in cybernautic missions, that is, expeditions through the environments of CD-ROMs, virtual reality, and the World Wide Web. Cybernautic missions performed with oral interfaces carry their own particular hazards, and not just those which human foods pose for machines.

Computers, for instance, can produce unsettling effects upon the human digestive system. Users of virtual reality sometimes suffer from "simulator sickness," a condition produced by immersion in cyberspace technologies. Its symptoms include eye discomfort, headaches, and, of particular interest to us, a strange nausea which can take two forms. This nausea fills some stomachs with the butterflies of an uncritical love of gadgetry. Others it coats with a chalky technological angst. Because this symptom affects so many cybernauts, Dr. La Morte has come to call it "cybernausea."

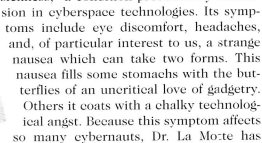

VReades will soon begin testing a group of nauseous cybernauts in order to address several critical questions. First, how do menus and order words produce the sensations of cybernausea, that is, gadget love and techno-angst? Alternatively, how to prepare cybernetic and existential ingredients for use in recipes which can transform this cybernausea into performances of becoming-wired? Finally, how to distinguish the flavors of orders and recipes, and what new sorts of evaluation may arise from the reformatted Java Drive?

In our initial tests, cybernauts will fly in VRcades' Virtual Vomit Comet, the world's first zero-gravity, fully immersive, flight simulator. Immersion consists of 3-dimensional graphics, stereo surround sound, and the Oral Joy Stick. A navigational device consisting of a polyurethane tube, the Oral Joy Stick is held in the teeth like a snorkel and comes equipped with respiratory, nutritional, and voice recognition systems, as well as a personal vomitory.

Conclusion

Cyber Space Foods will incorporate the flight tests from the Virtual Vomit Comet into its electronic taste tests and its study of cybernausea and the Java Drive. Using the data collected from these and other research areas, we hope to gain a greater sensitivity for oral interfaces and, in general, a more refined taste for human-computer feedback rituals. In what could stand as the motto for Cyber Space Foods, Dr. La Motte has summarized the approach we take toward interfacial performances by this paraphrase of Guattari: "One doesn't get to know electronic media through conceptual representation; rather, we must open ourselves to possibility of affective contamination." *Bon appetit.*

electronics

VRcades.

theory

entertainment

The Radiophonic Cookbook (excerpts)

Glazed Whisper Torte

his torte is meant to be broadcast after an early evening program of experimental music, but it is also a lovely way to surprise your listeners after an in-depth news show.

Preheat airwaves to suitable vibration.

Crust
4 cups flowers
water from the falls
 (if you do not live near a fall, you may pour the
water from a great height)
a teaspoon of tea
a tablespoon of table
1 birdsong, dolce e staccato
 (do not use the song of a migrating bird--it will
cause other ingredients to separate)

Place in proximity to a modern radio whose "seek" button has been pressed. As the station finder moves through the airwaves, the dough will roll itself out into the desired shape.

Filling
1 cup flutter
3 ounces murmur
2 eggs lightly bombasted
add quartz to taste

Take a deep breath. Do not stir too strenuously or whisper will become a scream. Pour into crust. Garnish with sighs.

Roasted Leg of Listen

This main course is perfect for broadcast during a festive season, or to perk up a dull musical rotation. Be sure you have a reliable neighborhood noise-butcher, since even the best radiophonic chef can do little with poor quality listen. Whether it is a whole large leg (interview, symphonic work, etc.), a boned and stuffed leg (DJ monologue, call-in radio show) or the short leg (10-spot, station identification), they all roast the same way regardless of timing.

SPECIAL NOTE

Cooking Levels for Listen

Cooking Stations. Always assess the station of the leg of listen at the radio with an instant listening thermometer, leaving it in the listen about 15 seconds so that it can register—once the listen is off the radio, the station reading will move some ten degrees up the dial as the ambient noises from the room circulate into the interior of the listen. (The following are live, on-air readings.)

88.5 FM	Very quiet
820 AM	Slightly quiet
96.5 FM	Moderate--speaking level
1040AM	Slightly loud

Timing. Because of its bulging shape and erratic movement, any leg of listen from 40 to 10 decibels will take 1 1/4 to 1 1/2 hours of roasting. Legs of 120 to 140 decibels may take 10 to 15 minutes longer.

Special Basting Sauce for Leg of Listen

This sauce can also be used for rack of hear, and, when in season, organic gossip. Never use gossip from the tabloids.

4 vicious rumors
(if the rumors are confirmed, use only 2)
1 rhyming couplet, lightly delivered
(if couplets are not in season, cut one out of a limerick and cover in lemon juice to keep from browning)
4 "Hey you!"
6 "Pardon me, Madame"
1 stick (4 ounces) lullaby

A note about vicious rumors. Vicious rumors are unpalatable raw. They are, however, more resilient when cooked than regular hearsay, which tends to dissipate when heated, and once cooked are quite savory.

Slowly melt the lullaby and brown slightly in a shallow sauce pan. Lay the vicious rumors flat in the lullaby and grate the "Hey you" and "Pardon me, Madame" on top. When rumors have gone slack and unsubstantiated, pour entire contents of sauce pan into blender and purée, gradually adding the rhyming couplet.

Halfway through cooking time, baste leg of listen every ten minutes until fully roasted. You will know when the leg is done because it will tell you in clear, dulcet tones.

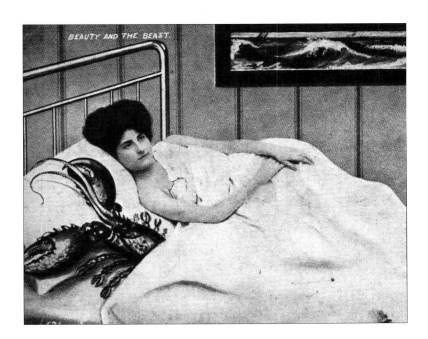

STREUSEL TOPPED FRUIT PIE

1 (9-inch) unbaked pastry shell*
2 (21-ounce) cans fruit pie filling (such as apple, cherry, strawberry, blueberry, peach or raspberry)
½ cup all-purpose flour
½ cup firmly packed Domino® Light Brown Sugar
¼ cup butter or margarine
½ cup chopped nuts (optional)

Preheat oven to 400°F.

Spoon pie filling into pastry shell.

In bowl, combine flour and brown sugar. Cut in butter until crumbly; stir in nuts. Crumble over pie filling. Bake 40 to 45 or until top is golden and filling is bubbly. Remove to wire cool. Makes 8 servings.

*If using a purchased frozen crust, buy a "deep dish" crust follow the basic guidelines on the package directions.

CANDIED SWEET POTATOES

2 (16-ounce) cans sweet potatoes in heavy syrup
½ cup firmly packed Domino® Light Brown Sugar
2 tablespoons butter or margarine
½ teaspoon grated orange rind
½ teaspoon ground cinnamon

Drain sweet potatoes, reserving ½ cup of the syrup. In large heat brown sugar, butter, orange rind, cinnamon and reserve to boiling. Reduce heat and simmer until slightly thickened 1 minute. Add sweet potatoes; heat through, gently stirring

NET WT. 10 OZ

Eve Jochnowitz

Notes from Home: Recipes, Menus and Cookbooks

Ravenous Reading: Recipes

I made cheesecake for the last meeting of my class today. Of course there was some extra batter that I baked in a small mixing bowl— your favorite part. It is on the top shelf of my refrigerator, if you want any.

A recipe for success. A recipe for disaster. The recipe form is an especially appealing much appropriated unit of prescriptive literature. There are numerous variations, especially in popular women's literature of something like "A recipe for a happy home": Take two cups of kindness, a pinch of understanding, and so on.

Considering the popularity of the recipe form, it is hard to understand the aesthetic and moral opprobrium in which actual recipes themselves are held. "I never use recipes," I have been told countless times. One of the first things many people say when they learn that I am a cook is "I bet you never use recipes." Of course I use recipes. What else? In fact I use recipes all the time. I read recipes more than I cook from them, and, more than that, I hoard them. You hate to let one slip through your fingers, even if you never intend to use it. I have piles and pile of slips cut from magazines and the backs of boxes, because the recipes might turn out to be just what I need. I have kept a copy of *Elvis Jesus and Coca-Cola* because it has a recipe for the King's Jello salad (Cherry Jello, Coca Cola, cream cheese, pineapple, white

195

grapes and pecans.[1] Neither the book nor the recipe has much to recommend it, but each makes the other more interesting.

Reading recipes is not like reading prose, and not everyone who can read can read recipes. It is more analogous to reading music. If you know the language, the recipes, and the music, play in your head. Once, for a period of about a year and a half, I could not read prose at all. My first marriage had just ended and without going into tedious detail, books, my oldest friends and constant companions, had, like my human friends, become complete strangers to me. I could not read more than a paragraph or so of prose without getting a hellish headache. I found that I could read recipes and I read recipes in bed, on the subway, under my desk at work and in all my available time. Recipe books that were particularly nourishing for me in my year without other literature were *Mastering the Art of French Cooking*[2] especially volume I; Madhur Jaffrey's *World of the East Vegetarian Cooking*[3] (I wrote Ms Jaffrey a gushing fan letter, for which I am embarrassed to this day); everything by Craig Claiborne and *Marlene Dietrich's A B C*, an autobiography in dictionary form by the actress.[4] This recipe for "Russian Salad (One of them)" is from her *A B C*. A good, spare, book with a handful of good, spare, recipes:

Russian Salad (One of them):

> Sliced apples, sliced tomatoes, sliced onions. Salt. Children like it without dressing. You can add oil and lemon, but no other kind of salad dressing. Serve it in large bowls. Makes a very good dinner with nothing else but cheese, bread and butter.

1. Friedman, Kinky. *Elvis Jesus and Coca-Cola* (New York: Bantam, 1993), p. 234.
2. Child, Julia, Louise Bertholle, and Simone Beck. *Mastering the Art of French Cooking* (New York: Knopf, 1983).
3. Madhur Jaffrey's *World of the East Vegetarian Cooking* (New York: Knopf, 1983).
4. Dietrich, Marlene. *Marlene Dietrich's A B C* (New York: Doubleday, 1962), p. 145

Bread and Wine: Menus and meals

> To all those who are about to hear and see the present report of the Official of the Paris Curia: we desire not to hide that a certain Jew living in Paris had a Christian maid from whom he bought a consecrated Host... He took up a large knife, struck at the Host... and it bled continuously (Chronicle of Jean de Thilrode, Hanover). quoted in Lavin).[1]

While it is not normally classed as a meal or a menu, the Holy Eucharist is both. It is a meal eaten in Catholic ceremonies re-enacting the Last Supper of Jesus, and it has a very specific menu, bread and wine. Of course they are more than bread and wine. The miracle of transubstantiation is the only time that the cooked, the baked bread, is turned into the raw, and in fact, living, body of Christ.

Because the consecrated Host is the actual Body of Jesus, mis-use of the Host is an enormous source of anxiety in both church and secular literature, particularly after the fourth Lateran Council of 1215, when the presence of Christ's body in the Host was made official Church doctrine. Legends of Eucharistic mir-acles tell of how a mistreated Host would reveal its divinity after having been desecrated out of stupidity and ignorance, usually by a woman, or out of viciousness and malice, always by a Jew. One of the more charming legends tells of a woman who stole a consecrated Host and put it in her beehives, hoping that it would increase her honey production. She learned her lesson the next morning when she saw that the bees had built a tiny alter, and were all kneeling (The bees' knees!) to worship the Host.[2]

Doing the wrong thing at a meal is a nightmare even when the stakes are much lower. A restaurant meal need not involve the supernatural to be a trial to the diners. Abraham Lincoln, it is said, was never so aware of his inferiority as when he was in the presence of a waiter.

Not all people, or all Presidents, are as sensitive about their behavior. In his memoirs of the Reagan white house, Mike Deaver recalls the disaster that resulted when Ronald and Nancy Reagan made a campaign appearance at an Episcopal Church. Deaver had not anticipated that Holy Communion, a ritual for-eign to the Reagans, would be part of the service. "Halfway down the aisle, I felt Nancy clutch my arm. 'Mike!' she hissed, 'Are those people drinking out of the same cup?'" Deaver assures

Nancy that she may simply dip the wafer in the wine, but she manages to lose her wafer in the wineglass. Reagan, having been ordered by his wife to 'do exactly as I do' dropped his in the wine as well, where it floated beside Mrs. Reagan's. "Nancy was relieved to leave the church. The President was chipper as he stepped into the sunlight, satisfied that the service had gone quite well."[3]

1. Lavin, Marilyn Aronberg. 1967. "The Altar of Corpus Domini in Urbino: Paolo Uccello, Joos Van Ghent, Piero della Francesca." In Art Bulletin 49, pp. 1-24.
2. Rubin, Miri. *Corpus Christi: The Eucharist in Late Medieval Culture.* (Cambridge: Cambridge University Press, 1991), pp. 123-124.
3. Didion, Joan. "Life at court. A review of Michael Deaver's book Behind the scenes and other books on the Reagans." *New York Review of Books,* 1989, December 21.

Place and Nation: Cookbooks

Today I was looking at my copy of the 1976 edition of *The Settlement Cookbook,*[1] a gift to me from your mother. Tomato soup. Oatmeal cookies. I just held it to feel its reassuring weight and thickness. This book is so yellow, this day so black.

Jochnowitz's Law: where there is contention, there is a cookbook. Neighborhoods and nations, faiths and families assert their presence and their identities in the publication of recipe collections, books so mundane and innocent-looking, that it is easy to forget their sympathetic power. A cookbook implies the existence of a cuisine, and the existence of a cuisine necessarily requires an intense and intimate connection between a people and a place. These connections usually go unremarked—you may read the cookbook or not, prepare the recipes or ignore them—but always, they remain. Soviet forces in Slovakia burned Ruthenian and Slovakian cookbooks along with other counter-revolutionary and nationalistic propaganda, in their attempts to Sovietize the region.[2] As tone deaf as they were on so many aesthetic issues, the Soviets recognized the danger in the music of regional cooking.

In Dubai, you can buy *Middle Eastern Cooking* by Jenny Ridgewell,[3] but censors will have diligently blacked out every recipe of Israeli origin before books are available for sale, in a

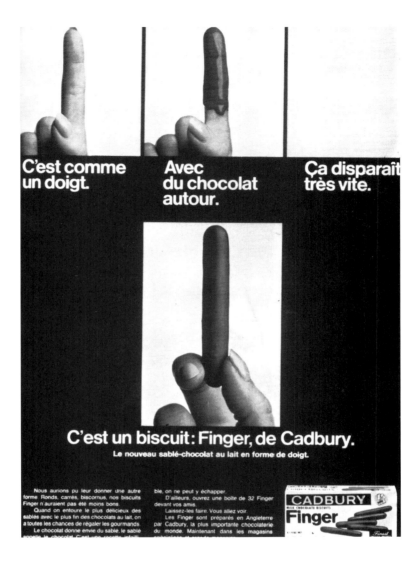

chilling attempt to obliterate the creativity of a people and the
people themselves. Don't think it can't happen here. *The
Complete Middle East Cookbook* by Tess Mallos[4] is an encyclo-
pedic collection of recipes, art, photography and other culinary
material from Greece, Cyprus, Turkey, Armenia, Syria,
Lebanon, Jordan, Iraq, Saudi Arabia, Gulf States, Yemen. Egypt,
Iran, Afganistan and Israel. In compliance with the Arab boycott
of Israel, however, the Australian publisher Weldon and Co.
agreed to censor all the material about Israel from the book, and

to remove a map of the region which included Israel from the endpapers of the original edition. The American publishers (McGraw Hill and then Tuttle) had no trouble going along with this culinary ethnic cleansing and all subsequent editions of *The Complete Middle East Cookbook* are not so complete.

1. *The Settlement Cookbook* (New York: Simon & Schuster, 3rd Ed., 1965, 1976).
2. Luard, Elizabeth. "Surviving the melting pot: Traditional feasts in Slovakia." Paper presented at Points of Contact: Performance Food and Cookery, Cardiff, Wales, January 1994.
3. Ridgewell, Jenny. *Middle Eastern Cooking* (London: Ward Lock, 1986).
4. Mallos, Tess. *The Complete Middle East Cookbook* (New York: McGraw Hill, 1979)
Reference: Carmel, Dalia. "The Middle East and cookbook censorship." Unpublished article courtesy of Ms. Carmel, 1991.

I saw red oak-leaf lettuce in the market today. I remember the first time I had it was when your father brought us some from his garden. God, it was delicious. I didn't think you would ever stop loving me.

Roxy Paine, *Dinner of the Dictators*, 1993-95. Freeze-dried food and place setting in glass table, 47-1/4 x 118-1/2 x 50 in. Photo Dennis Cowley.

Roxy Paine, *Dinner of the Dictators*, 1993-95. Freeze-dried food and place setting in glass table. Detail. Photo Dennis Cowley.

Roxy Paine, *Head Cheese (Small)*, 1995. Resin, auto body putty, and pigment, 20 x 23 x 1 in. Photo D. James Dee.

Roxy Paine, *Head Cheese (Large)*, 1995. Resin, auto body putty, and pigment, 46 x 55 x 1-1/2 in. Photo Dennis Cowley.

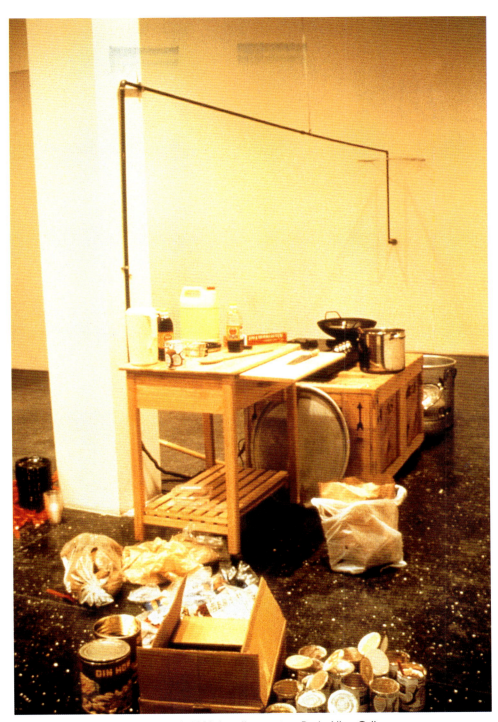

Rirkrit Tiravanija, *Untitled, (Pad Thai)*, 1990. Installation view, Paula Allen Gallery.

Rirkrit Tiravanija, *Untitled, (Cooking with Tang & Tim)*, 1993. Video tape, food, beer, lots of people. Wiener secession.

Rirkrit Tiravanija, *Bon Voyage Monsieur Akermann*, 1995. Courtesy Gavin Brown's Enterprise, NYC.

Robert Watts, *Tables and Neon Signature Environment*, Installation view. Bianchini Gallery, NYC, 1964-65.

Rober Watts, *Black Chop Dinner Table*, 1965. Plexiglass, photo laminates on wood, table, approx. 29 x 36 x 36 in. Collection Gino Di Maggio.

Robert Watts, *Laminated Dinner Table With Dinners and Floral Center Piece*, 1965. Color photographs laminated on wood, glass and wood table. 29 x 36 x 36 in.

Robert Watts, *White Chop Dinner Table*, 1965. Plexiglass, photo laminates, wood table, approx. 29 x 36 x 36 in. Collection Gino Di Maggio.

Robert Watts, *Laminated Dinner*, 1964-65. Color photos in plastic laminate, mounted on wood, approx. 15 x 15 x 3/4 in.

Robert Watts, *Placemat, Hand with Cigarette, Pea on Plate*, 1967. Black & white photographic print, 14 x 17 in.

Robert Watts, *Butter* 1964. Chrome, 2-1/4 x 7 x 2-3/4 in.

Robert Watts, *Cabbage*, 1964. Chrome plate on metal, plastic laminate on wood, 8 x 8-1/2 x 8-1/4 in.

Robert Watts, *Swiss Cheese on Plate*, 1964. Chrome, approx. 8 x 4 x 3/4 in. on 10 in. ceramic plate.

Robert Watts, *Pepper*, 1964. Chrome plate, approx. 7 x 4 x 5 in.

Rober Watts, *Chrome Cashews*, 1963. Chrome plate, glass jars, cashew nuts, 5 x 3 x 3 in. each. Collection Hermann Braun.

Robert Watts, *TV Dinner*, 1965. Laminated photographs mounted on wood, plastic casting for peas, 8 x 21 x 3/4 in.

Marcel Broodhaers, *Moules sauce blanche*, 1967. Painted iron pot, mussels, stained resin, 19-5/8 x 14-1/8 x 14-1/8 in. Courtesy Marian Goodman Gallery, NYC.

Perry Bard, 109. cut into julienne strips

Perry Bard, 111. strip of half a KKK face

Perry Bard, 106. skinheads with heads circled

Perry Bard, 101. Troy Murphy (head of KKK) with Halloween mask

Perry Bard, 96. skin a lemon

Perry Bard, 97. (b/w) KKK w. yellow square

From *Domestic Unrest*, 1996. Installation using video and slide projection that examines the aesthetics of violence, that place where, in the comfort of our own homes, ethnic cleansing becomes as palatable as coffee and a croissant. Images of neo-Nazis mix with a recipe for grandma's chicken soup, KKK members with lemon meringue pie. Southeast Museum of Photography, Daytona Beach, Florida.

"It's very provoking," Humpty Dumpty said after a long silence, looking away from Alice as he spoke, "to be called an egg,— very!"

Lewis Carroll
Through the Looking Glass

**"Narrow Escape"
by Maureen Connor**
is a video installation
that consists of a Neo-
Rococo armoire whose
three decorative panels
have been replaced with
video monitors. The
armoire is exhibited
with the set used for the
video's production. The
video begins with an
image of a 3-tiered plat-
ter of cakes and cookies
that are being surrepti-
tiously eaten. The image
on the center monitor
dissolves to show a
woman trying unsuc-
cessfully to fit into a
dress that is too small
for her. The next image is one
of the same woman trying to
enter a party through a door
that is very narrow, followed
by several others—all of whom
are quite slim. After managing
with some difficulty to pass
through this door, they find
that the chairs at the party are
also too narrow for even the
slimmest of them to sit on
comfortably. Then, when they
try to play musical chairs with
them they discover they are
too weak to support them as
well. Each time the music stops
and the women compete for
the remaining seats, one chair
after another collapses. Given
that no one is slim enough to
keep their chair intact, there
can be no winner. The moni-
tors to either side of the cen-
tral monitor show the women
as they exit the game eating
from the platters that began
the piece.

Contributors

George H. Bauer. At the time of his death, George Bauer was Professor of French at the University of Southern California. He was the author of *Sartre and the Artist,* (University of Chicago Press, 1969), as well as of numerous articles on Barthes, Duras, Sartre and Duchamp.

Jean-Claude Bonnet is editor of *La Carmagnole des Muses* (Armand Colin), and of Louis-Sebastien Mercier's *Le tableau de Paris* and *Le Nouveau Paris* (Mercure de France). He is Directeur de Recherche at the Centre National de la Recherche Scientifique.

Rodolphe el-Khoury is the co-author (with Rodolfo Machado) of *Monolithic Architecture* (Presto), and the translator of Jean-François de Bastide's *The Little House* (Princeton Architectural Press). He teaches at the Graduate School of Design of Harvard University.

Clayton Eschleman, poet, translator and critic, editor of *Sulfur,* one of the major poetry journals in the country, recipient of the National Book Award, Guggenheim Fellowship, NEA and NEH Grants; he has contributed to over 500 journals and anthologies; his translations from French and Spanish are classics.

Coco Fusco is a New York-based writer and interdisciplinary artist. She has lectured, performed, exhibited, and curated programs throughout the U.S., Europe, Canada, South Africa and Latin America. Her collection of essays on art, media and cultural politics, entitled *ENGLISH IS BROKEN HERE,* was recently published by The New Press.
Nao Bustamante is a writer, curator and performance artist pioneer who is originally from the San Joaquin Valley (Central California). Her performances have been presented in Mexico, Asia, Europe, Canada and the United States. Currently Nao is touring with Coco Fusco in their performance piece *STUFF.*
The text in this volume is the introduction to the following article: Coco Fusco and Nao Bustamante, 'STUFF,' *TDR/The Drama Review,* 41:4 (T156-Winter, 1997), forthcoming. ©1997 by New York University and the Massachusetts Institute of Technology.

Eve Jochnowitz, The Chocolate Lady, is cooking and foodways instructor at Living Tradition KlezKamp, New York correspondent of the Deli Project of the Magnes Museum and the author of "Eating the World: Foods of the United Nations" in *Food on the Move* (Prospect Books, 1997). She is a graduate student in the Department of Performance Studies, New York University.

Terri Kapsalis is a writer, performer, and health educator based in Chicago. She has recently published *Public Privates: Performing Gynecology from Both Ends of the Speculum* (Duke University Press, 1997).

Alexandra L.M. Keller is a doctoral candidate in Cinema Studies at New York University.

Alphonso Lingis, philosopher and translator, leading interpreter of continental philosophy in the USA, author of a dozen books, including the recent highly acclaimed *Abuses;* his work spans the cultural differences between European thought and the Third World, and has been cited as a major contribution to philosophy, religious studies and literary criticism.

Jon McKenzie is Project Director at VRcades and runs StudioLab, its digital performance workshop. His book, *Perform—or Else: Performance, Technology, and the Lecture Machine,* is forthcoming from Wesleyan University Press.

Mushim is writing a series of essays on Buddhist family practice and is working on *Zen Laundry*, a book-length memoir of her adventures in North American and Asian Buddhist monasteries. She lives with her partner and 8-year old son in Oakland, California.

Ron Scapp is director of the Graduate Program in Urban and Multicultural Education at the College of Mount Saint Vincent in the Bronx, New York. He is currently at work on a book, *A Question of Voice: The Search for Legitimacy.*

Richard Schechner, playwright, educator, theorist, Professor of Performance Studies at New York University, editor of *The Drama Review,* is a leading international figure in theater studies.

Lawrence R. Schehr is Professor of French at North Carolina State University. His books include *The Shock of Men; Alcibiades at the Door; Rendering French Realism;* and *Parts of an Andrology.* He is the co-editor, with Dominique Fisher, of *Articulations of Difference.*

Daniel Spoerri is an artist, author and chef, and one of the central figures associated with the Nouveaux Realistes. He is the author of *An anecdoted topography of chance* (Serpents Tail) and *Mythology & meatballs: a Greek island diary cookbook* (Aris Books).

Chantal Thomas is author of *La Reine scélélerate* (Le Seuil), *Thomas Bernard* (Le Seuil, 1990), *Sade* (Le Seuil, 1994), *La vie réelle des petites filles* (Gallimard, 1995). She is Directeur de Recherche at the Centre National de la Recherche Scientifique.

Lydia Vázquez is the author of *Elogio de la Seduccion y el Libertinaje* and the editor of *De lo Grotesco.* She is Professor of French Literature at the Universidad del País Vasco in Spain.

Jeff Weinstein is author of *Life in San Diego* (novella) and *Learning To Eat* (essays about food and eating), both published by Sun & Moon Press. He has written for *The New Yorker, Artforum, Art in America,* and many other publications. He was for 17 years restaurant critic for *The Village Voice.* He is now Fine Arts Editor of *The Philadelphia Inquirer.*

Allen Weiss is author of *Flamme et Festin: Une poétique de la cuisine* (Éditions Java); *Phantasmic Radio* (Duke); *Unnatural Horizons: Paradox and Contradiction in Landscape Architecture* (Princeton University Press). He teaches in the Department of Performance Studies at NYU.

Gregory Whitehead is a radio artist and writer; winner of the prestigious Prix Futura and the Prix Italia for his radio work. He is a native of Nantucket and fan of *Moby Dick,* thus his interest in writing for this volume of Lusitania on the poetry of chowders.

REPRESENTING THE LUXURY
LINER THE "HMS LUSITANIA"
THAT IN ITS DAY WAS ONE OF
THE GLORIES OF TECHNOLOGY
AND OPTIMISM, SINKING BENEATH
THE WAVES — A VICTIM OF SUPE-
RIOR TECHNOLOGIES — OUR
ANTHOLOGIES AND WEBSITE
HTTP://WWW.THING.NET/LUSITA-
NIA REFLECT THE SIMILAR DISSO-
LUTION OF MODERNIST
PREDILECTIONS UNDER THE PRES-
SURE OF THEIR OWN SUCCESSES
AND THE VIRTUAL FLOW OF NEW
ONES.

#6, VULVAMORPHIA

Vulvamorphia (vulva = wrapper, morphia = form), is an unusual collection of critical essays, fiction, experimental rebuses, and art works which navigates a broad spectrum of concepts from philosophy, architecture, anthropology, medical history, media analysis and cultural theory, lavishly illustrated with historical and contemporary artworks and photographs, in color and black and white.

A Vulvamorph sounds out a polyphonic chorus of little things, the sad, lost, discarded, forgotten, denied, repressed, disavowed and foreclosed subjects, objects, and thingnesses of the world.

Contributors include: Sandy Stone, "Invaginal Imaginal: How to Fill (Or Surround) Virtual Space"; Kristine Stiles, "Shaved Heads and Marked Bodies: Representations from Cultures of Trauma"; Christine Tamblyn, "Grafting Tentacles on the Octopussy"; Terry Kapsalis, "Vaginal Architecture"; Liz Kotz, "Beyond the Pleasure Principle"; and Alphonse Lingis, "Carnival in Rio."

Visual artists include: Louise Bourgeois, Carroll Dunham, Nicole Eisenman, Mary Heilmann, Beverly Semmes, Seton Smith, and Philip Taaff

In English and French.
Illustrated. 208 pages, 32 pgs in color.
ISBN: 1-882791-03-7 (1994) Paperback. $15

"Transgressive, inclusive, provocative and marginal, the vulvic space, the vulvamorphic, always insinuates itself as the liminal space for the germination/reformulation of a radical language that transforms visibly/passively the a-critical vacuum at the center of the Western gnoseological project: the space of feminized bodies, (...) of anything classified as a "thing" or de-subjectified.
The semantic, syntactic, and syntagmatic displacement required by a vulvamorphic writing, metamorphizes the language into a mimetic and performative organ, and is sometimes, at its best, highly self-ironic. In this way, it can be said that Lusitania's vulvamorphic issue fulfils itself in irony and intelligence."
—André Lepecki, in *Publico,* Lisbon, 1994

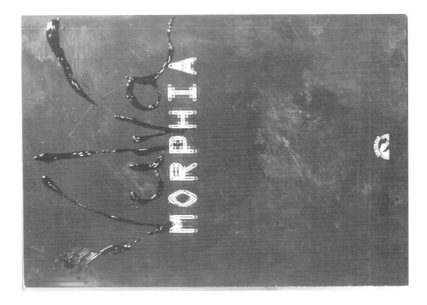

Sites and Stations: Provisional Utopias was conceived and edited by Stan Allen and Kyong Park, as an opportunity to re-think architecture, the city and culture, and the utopian project. The diverse texts map a broad range of issues and subjects, from the fantasy of Las Vegas to the real politics of urban planning. The contents of *Sites and Stations: Provisional Utopias* are organized under the headings "Technologies, Neo-realisms, Cartographies and Provisional Utopias." They slip between the personal meditations of Dan Hoffman's "Levittown Stories," reflecting on the effects of suburban planning and life in the fifties, to Alex Wall's view of "the American City and the Automobile," and Scott Bukatman's fantasy piece "Ann-Margret is my Co-pilot."

But all is not fun and games...

The realms of theory and cultural criticism are represented by Friedrich Kittler's observations on war and technology and its effects on urban design in his article "Expressway." *Sites and Stations* has two exclusive interviews, with Paul Virilio (by Enrique Limon) and Dave Hickey (by Stan Allen). In addition, articles by Jae Su Han ("The Future Lies in the Past"), Miwon Kwon ("Imagining an Impossible World Picture") and Aaron Tan ("The Walled City"), all address the effects of urbanism and modernization in Asia, from the point of view of the theoretical/personal (Kwon), the historical (Tan) and the theoretical (Han). Paralleling these, Kyong Park in his introduction, Celeste Olalquiaqa ("Paradise Lost") Thomas Bish and Hal Laessig ("Newark, the Hidden City"), represent the decay of the utopian dream of modernism and capitalism.

#7, SITES & STATIONS: PROVISIONAL UTOPIAS

Unwilling to just state the histories and problems of architects' utopian dreams in the age of declining expectations, *Sites and Stations* turns an eye to the optimism and pragmatics of

the utopian visions of such architects and artists as Enric Miralles ("Mollet del Vallés Park and Civic Center"), Langlands and Bell (by Adrian Dannatt), Jae Su Han, Hani Rashid and Anne Couture ("LAXNYCYHM: Urban Triptych") and Greg Lynn's "Projects." Many of these projects assert that it is in the territory of the image that architecture might work more effectively in recovering the new from a suspect vision of the utopian.

Illustrated. 256 pages, 32 in color.
ISBN: 1-882791-03-7 (1995)
Paperback. $15

On **Being On Line, Net Subjectivity:**

"...As always the choice of focus was just right as an intervention in today's cultural field."
Professor Norman Bryson
Harvard University

This anthology addresses the exciting new consciousness of the Internet, where identity is negotiated and love is the pleasure of the text. The contents range from sexually intense analyses of on-line writing to the "netwar" of the Zapatistas.

Edited by Alan Sondheim, *Being On Line, Net Subjectivity* is conceived as an exploration of the theory and practice of virtual identity as well as its effects. Unlike many recent books on the Internet, Being On Line focuses both on the promises of the technology and the actual content being developed by users of this form of exchange.

Intermixed with the esoteric ("Monogamousbody") and the absurd ("Are you a Cyborg?"), are topics ranging from subjectivity and community to the uncanny and netsex, presented in both theory and practice. Among the thirty-two authors are Angela Hunter, Ellen Zweig, and Nesta Stubbs; net feminist Doctress Neutopia; anthropologist Roger Bartra; and theorists Friedrich Kittler, Slavoj Zizek, Mark Poster and Gregory Ulmer. Being On Line is richly illustrated by artists whose works are related to virtual worlds. Four color sections present performance, graphics and sculpture by Regina Frank, Peter Halley, Mike Metz, and Alice Aycock. *Being On Line* includes Lusitania signature "editorial" in comic strip format.

Illustrated. 208 pages, 16 in color.
ISBN: 1-882791-04-5 (1996) Paperback. $15

On *City Lights'* Best Seller list in *Book Forum,* Fall, 1997.

#8, BEING ON LINE, NET SUBJECTIVITY

#10, 1962: A RECOUNTING

Lusitania's 10th anthology, *1962: A Recounting* focuses on events that made the year pivotal in the emerging crisis of the modernist world view.

With the triumph of mass culture and consumerism, 1962 marks the ascendancy of the "society of the spectacle" and sits squarely between the last gasps of postwar mop-up operations and the cultural revamping symbolized by the events of 1968.

1962 is "distinguished" by such events as the Cuban Missile Crisis, the march on Selma, Alabama, Adolphe Eichmann's trial and the intensification of the Space Race. It is also a significant moment in the transition from a world dominated by residual nineteenth century culture and politics to the emergence of "Global Village" technologies and the consolidation of corporate capital.

1962: A Recounting is organized around a full color, fold-out time-line of such crucial events as the development of mass media, the space race, anti-colonial struggles, civil rights, women's and anti-war movements, the New Wave, Situationists, Pop, Minimalism, and the challenge to Modernism's dominant theories and orthodoxies, illustrating the events, art and dynamics of the period 1961-1963. Edited by Saul Ostrow and Carole Ashley.

Illustrated, 208 pages, with 16-page pull-out center fold.
ISBN: 1-882791-06-1 (1998).
Paperback. $15

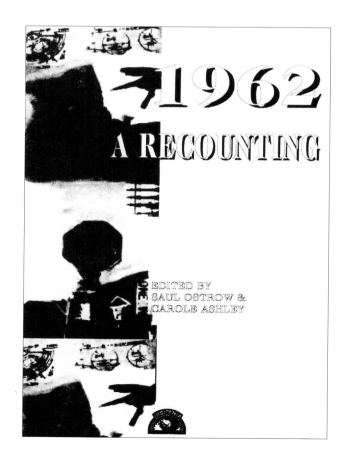

HOW TO ORDER

Cover price: $15.00

D.A.P./Distributed Art Publishers, Inc.
(Vols 8,9)
155 Sixth Avenue
New York, NY 10013-1507
Fax: 212-627-9484
Toll-Free: 1-800-338-BOOK

EUROPEAN DISTRIBUTION
Idea Books
Nieuwe Herengracht 11
10011 RK Amsterdam,
Netherlands
Tel: 31-20-622-6154
Fax: 020-620-9299

UK
Art Data
12 Bell Industrial Estate
50 Cunnington Street
London W4 5HB
Tel: 44-181-747-1061
Fax: 44-181-742-2319
email: artdata@btinternet.com

(Vols 4, 5, 6, 7):
AUTONOMEDIA
POB 568 Williamsburgh Station
Brooklyn, New York 11211-0568
Fax: 718-963-2603

Lusitania Press
104 Reade Street
New York, NY 10013
Fax: 212-732-3914
e-mail: Lusitania@thing.net
www.thing.net/lusitania

Black & white illustrations:

Page 6. Mount Street, Mayfair, London. Photo Mark Fiennes.

Page 41. Hokusai, *Dream of the Fisherman's Wife,* ca. 1820.

Page 42. Lucas Cranach (1472-1553), *Eve* (detail). Uffizi Gallery.

Page 68. Adam and Eve. Photo Frédéric Rolland

Pages 71 & 72. Carmen Miranda. Courtesy of the Academy of Motion Picture Arts and Sciences.

Page 97. Beach Party, 1950s. Photo Sante, Schwarm and Scheldon

Page 131. *Le Bonheur est Simple.* Photo Pierre Tairraz.

Page 153. Beato Angelico (1387-1455), *Institution of the Eucharist,* Museum of San Marco, Florence.

Parallax

a journal of metadiscursive theory and cultural practices

Editors
Joanne Morra and **Marquard Smith**
Centre for Cultural Studies, Department of Fine Art, University of Leeds, Leeds, LS2 9JT, UK
Email: parallax@leeds.ac.uk

Scope
Parallax is an exciting and provocative cultural studies journal which seeks to initiate alternative forms of cultural theory and criticism through a critical engagement with the production of cultural knowledges.

Parallax will be of interest to those working in many areas including critical theory, cultural history, gender studies, philosophy, queer theory, english and comparative literature, post-colonial theory, art history and of course, cultural studies.

Recent issues include

- cultural studies and philosophy
- theory and practice
- dissonant feminisms
- kojève's paris.now bataille

Subscription Information
Vol. 4 (1998), Quarterly
ISSN 1353-4645
Institutional: US$198/£120
Personal: US$58/£35

 Visit the Journal's Web Site
http://www.tandf.co.uk/

Sterling prices apply to UK subscribers only. Dollar prices apply to subscribers in all other countries. Personal subscriptions are available to home address only and must be paid for by personal cheque or credit card. All subscriptions are payable in advance and rates include postage. Payment may be made by cheque (Sterling or US Dollar), international money order, credit card or National Giro. EC Customers Please Note. All prices are excluding VAT

Now Published by Taylor & Francis

Free Email Contents Service

To sign up for our free contents service for this title, send an email to: mailserv@tandf.co.uk with *lists* in the body of the message to receive further instructions

Visit the T&F Web Site

http://www.tandf.co.uk/
or
http://tandfdc.com/

The Publishers

Taylor & Francis Publishers
1 Gunpowder Square
London, EC4A 3DE, UK
Tel: +44 (0) 171 583 0490
Fax: +44 (0) 171 583 0585
or
1900 Frost Road, Suite 101
Bristol, PA 19007-1598, USA
Tel: +1 800 821 8312
+1 215 785 5800
Fax: +1 215 785 5515

Email: info@tandf.co.uk
info@tandfpa.com

Free Sample Copies Available

JPLXAA4-0997

SARDELLENFILETS IN OEL
NONO
HERGESTELLT IN MAROKKO
Auch bei Kühlung nur begrenzt haltbar
SAINT LOUIS
pure canne
de Retz
ONO
PRODUIT PARFAIT
POUR LA
CONSERVATION
DES ŒUFS